THE Beauty OF HOLY CHOICES

Sarah J. Breese McCoy

WESTBOW
P R E S S®
A DIVISION OF THOMAS NELSON
& ZONDERVAN

Unless otherwise noted, all Scripture references in this book are taken from the King James Version, copyright © 1987/Crown. Used by permission of Public Domain in the United States.

WestBow Press books may be ordered through booksellers or by contacting:

WestBow Press
A Division of Thomas Nelson & Zondervan
1663 Liberty Drive
Bloomington, IN 47403
www.westbowpress.com
1 (866) 928-1240

ISBN: 978-1-5127-1475-3 (sc)
ISBN: 978-1-5127-1476-0 (hc)
ISBN: 978-1-5127-1474-6 (e)

Library of Congress Control Number: 2015916376

Print information available on the last page.

WestBow Press rev. date: 10/19/2015

CONTENTS

To my parents, Charles F. (Nick) and JoAnn Breese; my husband, Tom McCoy; and my six wonderful children, whose encouragement has made all the difference.

"Give unto the LORD the glory due unto his name: bring an offering, and come before him: worship the LORD in the *beauty of holiness*" (1 Chronicles 16:29, emphasis added).

"And when he had consulted with the people, he appointed singers unto the LORD, and that should praise the *beauty of holiness*, as they went out before the army, and to say, Praise the LORD; for his mercy endureth for ever" (2 Chronicles 20:21, emphasis added).

"Give unto the LORD the glory due unto his name; worship the LORD in the *beauty of holiness*" (Psalm 29:2, emphasis added).

"Thy people shall be willing in the day of thy power, in the *beauties of holiness* from the womb of the morning: thou hast the dew of thy youth" (Psalm 110:3, emphasis added).

INTRODUCTION

What common thread runs through a young women's pageant, an orange sunset behind a mountain range, the feel of top-quality silk, and the smell of home-baked bread? It is that people are naturally attracted to loveliness. Beauty draws us, makes us want to come sit awhile and take it all in, makes us want to somehow capture it for ourselves and incorporate it into our beings too.

The desire to experience beauty explains why we learn to play musical instruments, why we put out feeders that attract colorful birds to our yards, or why we go to nature preserves or buy paintings. It's why we wear perfume and get braces for our kids' crooked teeth. Get the picture? Loveliness is a joy to experience.

This book is about the most beautiful thing in all of the universe—the holiness of God and the righteous acts that naturally flow from that holiness. It stands in sharp contrast to the jaded caricature some people have in mind when they hear the word "holy." It is not a set of persnickety rules about what to wear, what to eat, or what to do. It is not a mere list of "don'ts" or some church lady's judgment about the motives of a fellow member. But defining holiness succinctly is a rather difficult thing to do, even for theologians. Not even the Bible spells out a concise definition for the word. Perhaps an analogy from Scripture can help.

One evening a Pharisee named Nicodemus visited Jesus because his heart was hungry for God. As Jesus explained to him about his need to be "born again," Jesus made an interesting statement about the Holy Spirit.

"The wind bloweth where it listeth, and thou hearest the sound thereof, but canst not tell whence it cometh, and whither it goeth: so is every one that is born of the Spirit" (John 3:8).

A holy choice, then, might be defined as doing the right thing, at the right time, for the right reason.

Although the Holy Spirit is not physically visible to us, his work is evident as people come to know Christ. In the same way, God's holiness is a fundamental characteristic of him, but it is usually only evidenced on earth indirectly by the righteous things God does and his absolute sinlessness. A pure heart is imparted to people when they accept Jesus as Savior, but it is maintained and evidenced outwardly by the proper choices they make and the righteous things they do. A holy choice, then, might be defined as doing the right thing, at the right time, for the right reason.

Human beings can't achieve holiness on their own. Isaiah said, "All our righteousness is like filthy rags" (Isaiah 64:4–9). Trying to be good without the covering of God's grace through Christ's blood is frustrating and futile. But that said, people are still responsible for what they decide to do. Some choices are evil, and some are righteous. The apostle Peter quoted the Jewish Torah when he wrote, "But just as he who called you is holy, so be holy in all you *do*; for it is written: 'Be holy, because I am holy'" (1 Peter 1:15-16, emphasis added); (Leviticus 11:44, 45; 19:2; 20:7). Sounds like Peter had some pretty high expectations of the people who called themselves Christ followers, didn't he? If what he wrote is truly God's anointed Word, then the command cannot be impossible. In fact, "with God all things are possible" (Matthew 19:26). God does not expect from us what he will not help us to do.

Want to be more attractive? Could you use a spiritual makeover perhaps? God's holiness is so awesome in its beauty that all creation is drawn toward it, and it would look just beautiful flowing through you. The Bible is filled with terrific stories about godly people who did the right thing in trying circumstances, and these stories explain various facets of God's holiness. The purpose of this book is to explore some of those key stories to gain inspiration for making righteous choices ourselves. Oh, to be more like this gorgeous God of ours!

CHAPTER 1

God Is Seated in the Temple

King Uzziah (also called Azariah) reigned over Judah for some fifty-two years, from about 799 to 748 BC. He was just sixteen years old at his coronation, and he was mostly good, as his father, Amaziah, and grandfather Joash had been (2 Kings 15; 2 Chronicles 26). During his reign, the prophet Isaiah was born, and the city of Rome was founded. Unfortunately, Uzziah overstepped his authority when he was about sixty-two by offering incense in the temple. The Torah expressly forbids anyone but the priests from doing this job (Numbers 16:40, 18:7), but Uzziah was prideful because he had been successful in a series of battles. When a company of eighty priests confronted him, Uzziah got angry. The Lord immediately struck him with leprosy, and from that day on, Uzziah lived in a leper colony while his son reigned in his stead.

Uzziah's death in 748 BC was the end of an era for Judah. Most of the population had never known any other king but him. He was a strong leader, a God-fearing man, a good organizer, and an advancer of technology (2 Chronicles 26:9–15). Sadly, when he should have been coming to the height of his glory, as his successes piled up and his wisdom grew, he blew it instead. His leprous body became repulsive, and he had to be quarantined with the other untouchables.

The same year that Uzziah was buried, the prophet Isaiah had a vision of another King. This King wasn't partly good and partly bad, like Uzziah had been. This King wasn't aging as time went by, growing weaker and sicker. This King was unbelievably glorious, and Isaiah was awestruck and even horrified by His holiness.

> In the year that king Uzziah died I saw also the Lord sitting upon a throne, high and lifted up, and his train filled the temple. Above it stood the seraphims: each one had six wings; with twain he covered his face, and with twain he covered his feet, and with twain he did fly. And one cried unto another, and said, Holy, holy, holy, is the Lord of hosts: the whole earth is full of his glory. And the posts of the door moved at the voice of him that cried, and the house was filled with smoke. Then said I, Woe is me! for I am undone; because I am a man of unclean lips, and I dwell in the midst of a people of unclean lips: for mine eyes have seen the King, the Lord of hosts. Then flew one of the seraphims unto me, having a live coal in his hand, which he had taken with the tongs from off the altar: And he laid it upon my mouth, and said, Lo, this hath touched thy lips; and thine iniquity is taken away, and thy sin purged. Also I heard the voice of the Lord, saying, Whom shall I send, and who will go for us? Then said I, Here am I; send me. (Isaiah 6:1–8)

God wears a robe? There's smoke in heaven? What could all this imagery mean? Isaiah has blessed us with a metaphor of

God's beautiful holiness. His creatures—whoever these servants called seraphs actually are—seem to be modest, for they cover their faces and their feet. Why would a sinless heavenly being use two wings to cover its face? Covering the face shields it from whatever it is exposed to and also keeps it from being viewed. We conclude that God's holiness is so glorious, so brilliant, and so full of energy that it's too much for the seraphs to bear directly. They must cover themselves.

Moses reacted in a similar way when he had an encounter with God at the burning bush in the Egyptian desert.

"And he said, Draw not nigh hither: put off thy shoes from off thy feet, for the place whereon thou standest is holy ground. Moreover he said, I am the God of thy father, the God of Abraham, the God of Isaac, and the God of Jacob. And Moses hid his face; for he was afraid to look upon God" (Exodus 3:5–6).

See what I'm talking about? Moses couldn't stand to look at God's majesty either. It was just too intensely fabulous to take in.

Back to Isaiah 6. Note the reaction of the seraphs to God's presence. Overwhelmed, all they could do was cry "Holy!" again and again. As people spontaneously say "ooh" and "ahh" at the beauty of fireworks in the sky on July 4, so the seraphs spontaneously reacted to God's beauty. The most fitting word that comes to their minds at this exciting time was *holy*!

John recorded a similar vision in his book of prophecy, Revelation.

> After this I looked, and, behold, a door was opened in heaven: and the first voice which I heard was as it were of a trumpet talking with me; which said, Come up hither, and I will shew thee things which must be hereafter. And immediately I was in the spirit: and, behold, a throne was set in heaven, and one sat on the throne. And he that sat was to look upon like a jasper and a sardine stone: and there was a rainbow round

about the throne, in sight like unto an emerald. And round about the throne were four and twenty seats: and upon the seats I saw four and twenty elders sitting, clothed in white raiment; and they had on their heads crowns of gold. And out of the throne proceeded lightnings and thunderings and voices: and there were seven lamps of fire burning before the throne, which are the seven Spirits of God. And before the throne there was a sea of glass like unto crystal: and in the midst of the throne, and round about the throne, were four beasts full of eyes before and behind. And the first beast was like a lion, and the second beast like a calf, and the third beast had a face as a man, and the fourth beast was like a flying eagle. And the four beasts had each of them six wings about him; and they were full of eyes within: and they rest not day and night, saying, Holy, holy, holy, Lord God Almighty, which was, and is, and is to come. And when those beasts give glory and honour and thanks to him that sat on the throne, who liveth for ever and ever, The four and twenty elders fall down before him that sat on the throne, and worship him that liveth for ever and ever, and cast their crowns before the throne, saying, Thou art worthy, O Lord, to receive glory and honour and power: for thou hast created all things, and for thy pleasure they are and were created. (Revelation 4:1–11)

See how the theme of beauty and holiness is repeated here, over eight hundred years after Isaiah's glimpse of heaven? God's appearance is likened to jasper and carnelian, which are both rich orange-red stones, warm like the color of fire and strong, rather than soft like a pastel. In like manner, other Scripture bears out the warmth and might of God, describing Him as a "consuming fire" (Hebrews 12:29) and our "strength" (Psalm 46:1).

John mentions a rainbow encircling the throne, but then he says it looked like an emerald (Revelation 4:3). Rainbows are a lovely display of all hues, and the brilliant green of the emerald is in the exact center of the visible light spectrum's order of color (remember your high school physical science—red, orange, yellow, *green*, blue, indigo, and violet). So John sees all the colors, yet he specifically mentions the one in the center. In the same way, John saw the entire throne room and all its occupants in heaven, but he was most focused on the beautiful, holy One in the center of it all.

How difficult and frustrating it must have been for John to attempt to describe that singular scene, because he knew that his readers would never really understand what he witnessed that day. But the words he uses repeatedly point to awesome beauty—sea of glass; blazing lamps; elders in white, wearing gold crowns. There with the Lord God are creatures unlike any living thing here on earth. Their response to the glory of the great One is to cry, "Holy!"

Would it not make sense to see someone like this and cry, "Beautiful"? Why, instead, the word *holy*? Perhaps it's because while there are many very beautiful things that are not necessarily perfect, anything holy *must* be *perfect* in beauty. So the creatures are describing a special kind of loveliness—flawlessness. Not only God's appearance but his very being, clear to the core, is without any fault at all and utterly beautiful beyond words. Oh, holy is the Lord!

Defining holiness as "without sin" may be technically accurate,

Not only God's appearance but his very being, clear to the core, is without any fault at all and utterly beautiful beyond words.

but somehow the true meaning is left wanting. It's easy to see from Scripture that God is holy (1 John 1:5), and that characteristic of his certainly means he's never done anything wrong. But also note that he's holy because *he's never neglected to do anything good that should be done.* James 4:17 says, "Therefore to him that knoweth to do good, and doeth it not, to him it is sin." God, who knows all things, certainly knows the good he ought to do. So if Scripture says clearly that he's never sinned, he must have always come through to do whatever should have been done.

Can you imagine a neglectful God who somehow doesn't quite get around to doing what he ought? Never! Even when we cannot understand why he didn't heal a loved one who suffered and passed away, or why he didn't remove the difficulties and barriers in someone's life, we can only conclude from his Word that God has always done all the good that he should have done. Put that with never doing anything bad or wrong, and what you have is quite simply beyond fabulous. God is altogether totally beautiful.

What earnest Christian wouldn't want to pattern himself after someone like that? The Bible is filled with examples of people who have done so, and you can learn from their successes. You can be like they were. You can be more like your heavenly Father than you've ever been before. Oh, to be holy! Lord, help us to be holy, as you are holy!

CHAPTER 2

Job Endures the Unimaginable

Job was probably the first book of the Bible ever written. Although the man Job likely lived at about the same time as Abraham, the writer of his book, whoever it was, recorded these events some five hundred years or so before Moses came along to write in the Law the events of creation, the story of Noah, and the other familiar things that happened first.

Somehow, Job knew about the one true God who made mankind. The Jewish people were not yet a nation—no synagogues or churches existed, and even the Ten Commandments had not yet been given—but Job had received enough word of mouth to know that God expected men to live in obedience to Him and that people of faith at that time offered animal sacrifices to the Lord when they sinned.

Job was the Bill Gates of his generation and culture. His wealth included thousands of domestic beasts of at least four species—a diversified portfolio of investments, if you will. Job had scores of employees to care for and manage his wealth. His wife bore him ten healthy children who all grew to adulthood in an age without modern conveniences or health care, and they had good relationships with each other. These brothers and sisters got along so well, in fact, that they had frequent reunions to celebrate special occasions.

Job cherished his kids and was concerned for their spiritual well-being. He interceded for them before God on a regular basis by offering sacrifices on an altar after every party they threw. He knew his children drank wine at these affairs, and he wanted to make sure everyone's behavior and heart attitudes were covered by God's grace. Job was the quintessential "what a guy."

Now for some extra-interesting insight.

"Now there was a day when the sons of God came to present themselves before the Lord, and Satan came also among them" (Job 1:6).

In that other dimension, where spiritual beings dwell, Satan sought interaction with God. Who knew that God permitted Satan to come and address him at the Lord's discretion? Although Satan had been cast out of God's presence and down to earth (Luke 10:18) for God's own purposes, God apparently still allowed "that old serpent" (Revelation 20:2) to access him, at least from time to time. In fact, once Satan showed up, it was God who initiated the conversation:

> And the Lord said unto Satan, Whence comest thou? Then Satan answered the Lord, and said, From going to and fro in the earth, and from walking up and down in it. And the Lord said unto Satan, Hast thou considered my servant Job, that there is none like him in the earth, a perfect and an upright man, one that feareth God, and escheweth evil? Then Satan answered the Lord, and said, Doth Job fear God for nought? Hast not thou made an hedge about him, and about his house, and about all that he hath on every

side? thou hast blessed the work of his hands, and his substance is increased in the land. But put forth thine hand now, and touch all that he hath, and he will curse thee to thy face. And the Lord said unto Satan, Behold, all that he hath is in thy power; only upon himself put not forth thine hand. So Satan went forth from the presence of the Lord. (Job 1:7–12)

For our understanding, this communication is presented as a regular back-and-forth dialogue that used spoken language. Whatever it actually was on the spiritual level, one thing is clear: God gave Satan permission to afflict Job but also laid some ground rules about how far Satan could go. Job was to be put to the test.

Sometime later, Job lost nearly everything he owned and all ten of his children in *one day*. Two enemy armies cruelly murdered servants and stole all his donkeys, oxen, and camels. "Fire from the sky"—perhaps a severe thunderstorm with lightning that caused a fire—killed all of the sheep. A tornado of some sort, perhaps spawned by the same thunderstorm, struck the house where his children were partying, wiping them all out as walls collapsed on them. Job is left to try to comprehend a tragedy so large that it can only be likened to the worst war trauma or the most horrific torture scenes that human history records.

Numb and probably on autopilot, Job's response is awe-inspiring.

"Then Job arose, and rent his mantle, and shaved his head, and fell down upon the ground, and worshipped, And said, Naked came I out of my mother's womb, and naked shall I return thither: the Lord gave, and the Lord hath taken away; blessed be the name of the Lord. In all this Job sinned not, nor charged God foolishly" (Job 1:20–22).

Job worshipped. He lost everything; he had no idea why. He could not even fully comprehend what had just happened, and his stress level was literally off the charts. *And Job worshipped.* But wait. There's more!

> Again there was a day when the sons of God came to present themselves before the Lord, and Satan came also among them to present himself before the Lord. And the Lord said unto Satan, From whence comest thou? And Satan answered the Lord, and said, From going to and fro in the earth, and from walking up and down in it. And the Lord said unto Satan, Hast thou considered my servant Job, that there is none like him in the earth, a perfect and an upright man, one that feareth God, and escheweth evil? and still he holdeth fast his integrity, although thou movedst me against him, to destroy him without cause. And Satan answered the Lord, and said, Skin for skin, yea, all that a man hath will he give for his life. But put forth thine hand now, and touch his bone and his flesh, and he will curse thee to thy face. And the Lord said unto Satan, Behold, he is in thine hand; but save his life. So went Satan forth from the presence of the Lord, and smote Job with sore boils from the sole of his foot unto his crown. And he took him a potsherd to scrape himself withal; and he sat down among the ashes. Then said his wife unto him, Dost thou still retain thine integrity? curse God, and die. (Job 2:1–9)

Job's losing his possessions and *all* of his children was not enough of a test, somehow. Satan then received permission from God to go to the brink of Job's very life and rob him of his health and physical appearance. Job was a horrified shell of a broken man, filled with a gross infection that he felt compelled to scrape. Job literally had nothing left but the roof over his head and his wife.

But Job's poor wife had been through all the same tragedies as he had, save the loss of her health. All *her* children were dead too. All her wealth was down the drain, the employees were nearly all gone, and her once-healthy husband was this pitiful, unrecognizable, sick, grotesque-looking man.

Mrs. Job just couldn't take it anymore, and she desperately wanted out. She must have thought, *If only he would die, I could run away and forget I ever knew him.* She had seen how he had lived the best life of faith he could, and it didn't seem to be enough for God. Tragedy struck anyway. So she wasn't interested in hanging on to God either. She wanted out—and that meant rejecting her husband.

Job's response to her rejection is nearly unbelievable. "But he said unto her, Thou speakest as one of the foolish women speaketh. What? shall we receive good at the hand of God, and shall we not receive evil? In all this did not Job sin with his lips" (Job 2:10).

This book is about holiness, remember? Can you see the beauty of this righteous response? Can you feel the glory of the right choice Job made, even though he couldn't see what God was doing and had no idea why this was happening to him?

The apostle Paul mentioned the value of endurance to his protégé, Timothy, and also to the church in Ephesus. "Thou therefore endure hardness, as a good soldier of Jesus Christ" (2 Timothy 2:3).

"Wherefore take unto you the whole armour of God, that ye may be able to withstand in the evil day, and having done all, to stand" (Ephesians 6:13).

Sounds like Job, doesn't it? He had nothing left that he could do but simply stand in the wind and let it blow.

Jesus made an interesting statement that connects holy endurance to salvation itself. "And ye shall be hated of all men for my name's sake: but he that endureth to the end shall be saved" (Matthew 10:22).

Holy endurance lasts until. It is there as long as needed, no matter how difficult the situation.

Holy endurance lasts *until*. It is there as long as needed, no matter how difficult the situation. This endurance has served Christians well when they have had to care for terminally ill family members for months on end, when they've languished in a prison cell in solitary confinement for spreading the gospel, and when they've encountered numerous setbacks and opposition on the mission field. It even works when you've lost your job and the search for another one goes on and on and on. God seems to be saying, "When times are hard, stand there and take it. You can do it because I'm with you."

The thing is that hard times don't last forever. Job found out that a great reward awaited him on the other side of his trial.

> After Job had prayed for his friends, the LORD made him prosperous again and gave him twice as much as he had before. All his brothers and sisters and everyone who had known him before came and ate with him in his house. They comforted and consoled him over all the trouble the LORD had brought upon him, and each one gave him a piece of silver and a gold ring. The LORD blessed the latter part of Job's life more than the first. He had fourteen thousand sheep, six thousand camels, a thousand yoke of oxen and a thousand donkeys. And he also had seven sons

and three daughters. The first daughter he named Jemimah, the second Keziah and the third Keren-Happuch. Nowhere in all the land were there found women as beautiful as Job's daughters, and their father granted them an inheritance along with their brothers. After this, Job lived a hundred and forty years; he saw his children and their children to the fourth generation. And so he died, old and full of years. (Job 42:10–17)

Getting his stuff back and having more children weren't even the best parts. For thousands of years since this trial occurred, people have been reading about it in God's Word and have been inspired to keep going when bad things happen to good people. They've been taught to trust when life isn't fair. No one told Job about that outcome at the time. No angel from heaven tapped him on the shoulder and said, "Hey, Job, we know this is really hard for you, but just hang on, because God's plan is to use your good example to help billions of people over thousands of years." Instead, the only sound from heaven was ... silence (cue chirping crickets).

How holy and beautiful is this endurance.

"Take, my brethren, the prophets, who have spoken in the name of the Lord, for an example of suffering affliction, and of patience. Behold, we count them happy which endure. Ye have heard of the patience of Job, and have seen the end of the Lord; that the Lord is very pitiful, and of tender mercy" (James 5:10–11).

Three things stand about Job's endurance. First, as he white-knuckled his way through the misery; he never felt entitled to God's blessings.

"Then Job arose, and rent his mantle, and shaved his head, and fell down upon the ground, and worshipped, And said, Naked came I out of my mother's womb, and naked shall I return thither: the Lord gave, and the Lord hath taken away; blessed be the name of the Lord" (Job 1:20–21).

"What? shall we receive good at the hand of God, and shall we not receive evil?" (Job 2:10).

Job's attitude was that God owed him nothing. He was not indignant. There was no "How dare God do this to me when I've been so faithful?" He was frustrated, and he did question. But he did not insist that God owed him one. Lovely.

Second, Job stayed true to God, regardless of the circumstances. He wasn't a "fair-weather follower."

"Then Job arose, and rent his mantle, and shaved his head, and fell down upon the ground, and worshipped, And said, Naked came I out of my mother's womb, and naked shall I return thither: the Lord gave, and the Lord hath taken away; blessed be the name of the Lord" (Job 1:20–21).

Instead of "This stinks, and I'm outta here," Job stayed with God. No fist-shaking at the sky; no railing about God's unfairness. He was as solid as a rock. He had nothing left, not even a wife or his own health, but he stayed the course. Gorgeous.

Third, Job did not accuse God of foolish behavior.

"In all this Job sinned not, nor charged God foolishly" (Job 1:22).

It would be easy to be short-sighted and sure that God had blown it. But Job didn't give in to the temptation to look at things that way.

One last observation: in the midst of it all, when Job was pouring out his heart to his friends in agony and frustration as he searched for a "why" that wasn't becoming clear, he made an incredible statement.

"Oh that my words were now written! oh that they were printed in a book! That they were graven with an iron pen and lead in the rock for ever! For I know that my redeemer liveth, and that he shall stand at the latter day upon the earth: And though after my skin worms destroy this body, yet in my flesh shall I see God: Whom I shall see for myself, and mine eyes shall behold, and not another; though my reins be consumed within me" (Job 19:23–27).

Turns out his words *were* recorded and written on a scroll, engraved in rock forever! God's Word endures for eternity (1 Peter 1:25), and Job's cries made it into the Book of books! The yearning, the pain, the grief, and the abandonment didn't last so very long. But the beauty of the holy endurance that Job displayed in an extraordinarily difficult trial will live on, even long after our present era is past.

Want to look beautiful? You can put on this same holiness by enduring through hardship, without wavering in your trust that God sees and will bring you through. Jesus Christ himself also endured until he came through victorious on the other side, remember? And he's one beautiful Savior.

Maybe you've been through a gut-wrenching divorce. Maybe you're in financial crisis or suffering with rebellious kids or warring in-laws. Maybe getting up and going to work every day feels like torture. Job endured, and you can too. If you'll keep going, God will bring you out on the other side. This hard time is not destined to last forever. Walk through it. Walk with him, and never, ever quit.

CHAPTER 3

Joseph Shows Self-Control

Abraham's grandson Jacob had thirteen children by four women—two wives (who were sisters) and two concubines (the two sisters' maids). Twelve of the kids were boys, and one boy in particular, Joseph, was Jacob's very favorite. Jacob, who was later renamed Israel by God, loved his son Joseph best for at least a couple of reasons. First, Joseph's mother was Jacob's beloved Rachel, the one he'd had to work fourteen years for to get permission from her father to wed her. Jacob was a decent man, and he was good to the other wife and concubines, but they didn't really have his heart as Rachel did.

The second reason why Jacob loved Joseph best was that his beloved Rachel had struggled with infertility for years and years after they married, and the tears and frustration she felt as the rival women produced offspring became almost too much for her to bear. When God finally answered Jacob's prayer and Rachel became pregnant, Jacob was getting on in years. He'd mellowed and relaxed and could enjoy his son, perhaps more than when he was younger, busier with his flocks and herds, and more driven.

Joseph liked being the favorite, and he wasn't above rubbing his brothers' noses in it. They became especially jealous when their dad made Joseph a colorful coat, and when Joseph reported to them that he'd had a dream about their someday bowing down to him. So when Joseph was sent out to the wilderness to check on his brothers as they grazed their livestock, they sold him as a slave to a caravan of people headed for Egypt. They then told their father that he'd been killed by wild animals. Joseph started his new life in Egypt as a slave.

And Joseph was brought down to Egypt; and Potiphar, an officer of Pharaoh, captain of the guard, an Egyptian, bought him of the hands of the Ishmeelites, which had brought him down thither. And the Lord was with Joseph, and he was a prosperous man; and he was in the house of his master the Egyptian. And his master saw that the Lord was with him, and that the Lord made all that he did to prosper in his hand. And Joseph found grace in his sight, and he served him: and he made him overseer over his house, and all that he had he put into his hand. And it came to pass from the time that he had made him overseer in his house, and over all that he had, that the Lord blessed the Egyptian's house for Joseph's sake; and the blessing of the Lord was upon all that he had in the house, and in the field. And he left all that he had in Joseph's hand; and he knew not ought he had, save the bread which he did eat. And Joseph was a goodly person, and well favoured. And it came to pass after these things, that his master's wife cast her eyes upon Joseph; and she said, Lie with me. But he refused, and said unto his master's wife, Behold, my master wotteth not what is with me in the house, and he hath committed all that he hath to my hand; There is none greater in this house than I; neither hath he kept back any thing from me but thee, because thou art his wife: how then can I do this great wickedness, and sin against God? And it came to pass, as she spake to Joseph day by day, that he hearkened not unto her, to lie by her, or to be with her. And it came to pass about this time, that Joseph went into the house to do his business; and there was none of the men of the house there within. And she caught him by his garment, saying, Lie with me: and he left his garment in her hand, and fled, and got him out. And it came to pass, when she saw that he had left his garment in her hand, and was fled forth, That she called unto the men of her house, and spake unto them, saying, See, he hath brought in an Hebrew unto us to mock us; he came in unto me to lie with me, and I cried with a loud voice: And it came to pass, when he heard that I lifted up my voice and cried, that he left his garment with me, and fled, and got him out. And she laid up his garment by her, until his lord came home. And she spake unto him according to these words, saying, The Hebrew servant, which thou hast brought unto us, came in unto me to mock me: And it came to pass, as I lifted up my voice and cried, that he left his garment with me, and fled out. And it came to pass, when his master heard the words of his wife, which she spake unto him, saying, After this manner did thy servant to me; that his wrath was kindled. And Joseph's master took him, and put him into the prison, a place where the king's prisoners were bound: and he was there in the prison. But the Lord was with Joseph, and shewed him mercy, and gave him favour in the sight of the keeper of the prison. And the keeper of the prison committed to Joseph's hand all the prisoners that were in the prison; and whatsoever they did there, he was the doer of it. The keeper of the prison looked not to any thing that was under his hand; because the Lord was with him, and that which he did, the Lord made it to prosper. (Genesis 39:1–23)

And Pharaoh said unto Joseph, Forasmuch as God hath shewed thee all this, there is none so discreet and wise as thou art: Thou shalt be over my house, and according unto thy word shall all my people be ruled: only in the throne will I be greater than thou. And Pharaoh said unto Joseph, See, I have set thee over all the land of Egypt. And Pharaoh took off his ring from his hand, and put it upon Joseph's hand, and arrayed him in vestures of fine linen, and put a gold chain about his neck; And he made him to ride in the second chariot which he had; and they cried before him, Bow the knee: and he made him ruler over all the land of Egypt. And Pharaoh said unto Joseph, I am Pharaoh, and without thee shall no man lift up his hand or foot in all the land of Egypt. And Pharaoh called Joseph's name Zaphnathpaaneah; and he gave him to wife Asenath the daughter of Potipherah priest of On. And Joseph went out over all the land of Egypt. And Joseph was thirty years old when he stood before Pharaoh king of Egypt. And Joseph went out from the presence of Pharaoh, and went throughout all the land of Egypt. And in the seven plenteous years the earth brought forth by handfuls. And he gathered up all the food of the seven years, which were in the land of Egypt, and laid up the food in the cities: the food of the field, which was round about every city, laid he up in the same. And Joseph gathered corn as the sand of the sea, very much, until he left numbering; for it was without number. And unto Joseph were born two sons before the years of famine came, which Asenath the daughter of

Potipherah priest of On bare unto him. And Joseph called the name of the firstborn Manasseh: For God, said he, hath made me forget all my toil, and all my father's house. And the name of the second called he Ephraim: For God hath caused me to be fruitful in the land of my affliction. (Genesis 41:39–52)

Joseph was apparently in his late teens or early twenties when this temptation from Potiphar's wife came his way, the time in life when a man's sex drive and testosterone levels are typically higher than at any other age. Joseph was not married, and he had no girlfriend. In fact, he had no prospect of a legitimate sex life at any time in his foreseeable future. For all he knew (save for the faith he had in his previous dream), he would always be someone's slave. On the other hand, Potiphar was a rich man who was used to having whatever his heart desired. It is unlikely that his wife was anything other than beautiful— veritable "arm candy," with maidservants to wait on her, dress her in the finest, coif her hair, and put on her makeup.

It would be naïve to believe that Joseph was put off by Potiphar's wife and not attracted to her. Why would Satan put a temptation in Joseph's way to trip him up and thwart God's plan for his people unless it was truly an enticing thing, difficult to resist? Joseph knew that Potiphar wasn't paying a lot of attention, and he knew when Potiphar wasn't around. Surely the thought of the pleasures of an affair with his boss's wife came to his mind, again and again. "No one will ever know," the tempter's voice must have whispered. "You have to do what she says anyway. She's your boss. You can't control this. Just enjoy it. You'll probably always be a slave anyway. Imagine the extra perks that could come your way if you sleep with her."

How is it possible to ever say no when faced with something so alluring? Does the Bible say anything at all about *how* to face temptation, or does it mostly just say not to do certain things?

Actually, the Bible does lay out two main strategies for facing temptation, and Joseph used them both. They are tried and true, and these holy choices can work for you too, whether you feel the urge to overeat, cheat on your taxes, or simply be lazy and neglect your responsibilities. I like to call the strategies "fight or flight."

Remember the "fight-or-flight syndrome" from biology class? Whenever you're faced with some sort of threat, the body's adrenal organs release a hormone called adrenaline (or epinephrine) into the bloodstream. It prepares you to cope with the emergency, either by (1) staying and fighting, or (2) running away, if it is possible to do so.

Staying and Fighting

When Joseph was faced with Mrs. Potiphar's suggestions day after day, he stood his ground and fought. The apostle Paul describes such a battle well in his first letter to the Corinthians. "Know ye not that they which run in a race run all, but one receiveth the prize? So run, that ye may obtain. And every man that striveth for the mastery is temperate in all things. Now they do it to obtain a corruptible crown; but we an incorruptible. I therefore so run, not as uncertainly; so fight I, not as one that beateth the air: But I keep under my body, and bring it into subjection: lest that by any means, when I have preached to others, I myself should be a castaway" (Corinthians 9:24–27).

He uses the word "fight" in Corinthians 9:26 and talks about the struggle to bring his own flesh into submission. In the same way, Joseph made up his mind. There were certain lines he wasn't going to cross and certain things he just wasn't going to do. Period. So when he had to, he stood his ground and fought the urge as though he were in a wrestling match.

Sometimes when people fight, they use weapons, and in Paul's day a formidable weapon of choice was the sword. A sharp one could pierce the belly of the enemy and destroy him in a minute. When Paul wrote his famous passage about the armor of God to the church in Ephesus, he was careful to describe a weapon God gives us for use against our enemy, Satan:

"Finally, my brethren, be strong in the Lord, and in the power of his might. Put on the whole armour of God, that ye may be able to stand against the wiles of the devil ... And take the helmet of salvation, and the sword of the Spirit, which is the word of God" (Ephesians 6:10, 11, 17).

The Bible, or God's Word, is the ultimate weapon in the defeat of temptation. Even though none of the Old Testament had yet been written in Joseph's day, God's expectations were passed down orally and were written within the hearts of people of conscience. Joseph knew that adultery was displeasing to the Lord, and he affirmed it when he said to Potiphar's wife, "How then can I do this great wickedness, and sin against God?" (Genesis 39:9).

So even without access to explicit instructions about how to fight this battle of temptation, Joseph sensed that he needed to voice the truth that adultery is against the sacred Law of God. When he did so, he struck a blow for righteousness and won the battle, if not yet the war.

Jesus used the Word of God to fight the awful temptations that Satan brought his way after forty days of fasting in the desert. All three times, recorded in both Matthew 4 and Luke 4, Jesus begins his retort to Satan by quoting God's Law from the Torah, which was given to Moses. That Word was powerful enough to defeat the temptation Jesus had to turn stones to bread when he was at the point of starvation. Don't you think that Word can help you too?

Running Away When Possible

Not every battle must be fought. Why engage if you can simply absent yourself from the difficulty? For example, if overeating is your weakness, wouldn't it be far better to simply make sure there are no junk foods in your house than to buy them and then try to fight the urge to open a bag of chips and eat the whole thing?

Joseph's ultimate test came when Potiphar's wife got bold enough and desperate enough to actually lay her hands on him.

"And she caught him by his garment, saying, Lie with me: and he left his garment in her hand, and fled, and got him out" (Genesis 39:12).

There was no talking himself out of this one. If Joseph had started another speech about how adultery is sinful, Mrs. Potiphar would probably have just ignored it and kissed him. No, this time, Joseph had to run like crazy—even if it meant leaving his coat behind in the hands of his boss's wife. You will have chances to get away from some of your biggest temptations too. Always leave, if you can.

When tempting Christ, Satan saved the greatest test for last.

"Again, the devil taketh him up into an exceeding high mountain, and sheweth him all the kingdoms of the world, and the glory of them; And saith unto him, All these things will I give thee, if thou wilt fall down and worship me. Then saith Jesus unto him, Get thee hence, Satan: for it is written, Thou shalt worship the Lord thy God, and him only shalt thou serve" (Matthew 4:8–10).

Jesus still stood and fought with the sword of the Spirit, which is the Word of God, as he had done before. But by this time, he'd had enough. He effectively fled the situation by commanding the Devil to get out. The words "away from me!" accomplished what running away would have, if Christ's temptation had been dependent on a thing or a location in space. The way to get away from it all was to make Satan go. And go he did.

Paul echoes the running-away strategy in his advice to Timothy: "Flee also youthful lusts: but follow righteousness, faith, charity, peace, with them that call on the Lord out of a pure heart" (2 Timothy 2:22).

Paul says "flee" and adds a nice extra by telling Timothy to run *toward* something as well. "Flee evil" and "pursue righteousness" work awfully well together.

Oh, the beauty of a character that refuses to do the wrong thing, even when it is oh-so-appealing!

But back to holiness. As giving in to temptation is sin, resisting temptation is a holy choice. Oh, the beauty of a character that refuses to do the wrong thing, even when it is oh-so-appealing! How pleasing the personality of someone who has made up his mind to resist what he knows is sin! Will you fight and flee as needed? Will you study God's Word and memorize it, so that you have a ready weapon when the opportunity to sin is before you?

CHAPTER 4

Puah and Shiprah Respect Life

After Jacob's son Joseph served as a slave in Egypt, God eventually raised him up to a position of power that was second only to Pharaoh, and Joseph's extended family joined him there during a severe famine. Generations later, the children of Israel were still living on the outskirts of Pharaoh's capital city in the land of Goshen, where they took care of their herds. As God blessed them and they grew, they somehow seemed ominous and threatening to Egypt's new ruler, so he enslaved them to preempt a coup.

The once-happy family became bowed down with hard labor and angry taskmasters as they made brick to build the pyramids. Yet instead of their fertility suffering, it thrived. Many young Jewish women continually gave birth to healthy baby boys and girls who survived. Finally, Pharaoh had had enough.

"And the king of Egypt spake to the Hebrew midwives, of which the name of the one was Shiphrah, and the name of the other Puah: And he said, When ye do the office of a midwife to the Hebrew women, and see them upon the stools; if it be a son, then ye shall kill him: but if it be a daughter, then she shall live" (Exodus 1:15–16).

Pharaoh decided to practice a draconian form of population control—infanticide. He figured the best time to do the deed was right at birth, before the mother ever had the chance to hold or suckle her child. Just tuck the newborn under an arm, bolt out the door, and toss it into the Nile, while the mother was not in any position to resist and before she could see or bond with her baby. It was a slash-and-burn mentality, devoid of compassion and designed for utmost efficiency.

Puah and Shiprah both had made a career of helping to bring life into the world. Perhaps their skills had prevented many stillbirths and maternal deaths. At the very least, they were coaches and comforters, assistants, and a loving set of extra hands when a new mother needed it most. It is not reasonable to assume that only two women could handle the childbirth needs of a population that may have been a half million or more at this point. Dozens of babies would have been born every day, especially in an age without much, if any, contraception. However, it does appear that any other midwives who delivered Hebrew babies at that time were under the direction of Puah and Shiprah. That's why Pharaoh addressed them specifically. You could think of these women as the chief attending obstetricians of their day.

Can you even begin to imagine the dilemma in which these midwives were placed? It was, quite simply, "Kill or be killed." No one stood up to Pharaoh and refused to obey his commands, even on moral grounds. It wasn't doable. He'd simply nod to his right-hand man, and the person's life would be over—just like that.

Perhaps the women contemplated, for just a minute, what it would mean to obey the king. "We wouldn't even have to let the baby ever take its first breath," they may have thought. "We could just tell the mom the baby wasn't born alive, and she'd have no way of knowing for sure. God will understand. Our lives are at stake here."

However, the holy choice is often the difficult one. There is no acceptable justification for the murder of someone's newborn, not even to preserve your own life. You simply have to stand in the wind without getting blown over and say, "No, I will not do this, no matter what." And that is exactly what these ladies did.

You simply have to stand in the wind without getting blown over and say, "No, I will not do this, no matter what."

So the days went by, and nothing changed about their delivery routine. When a beautiful baby boy let out his first cry, Puah and Shiprah rejoiced with the family. They dried the baby off, cut the cord, cleaned out his mouth, wrapped him up, and placed him with his mother. Perhaps they were a little nervous now and then, but they never wavered. They were midwives, not murderers.

"But the midwives feared God, and did not as the king of Egypt commanded them, but saved the men children alive. And the king of Egypt called for the midwives, and said unto them, Why have ye done this thing, and have saved the men children alive? And the midwives said unto Pharaoh, Because the Hebrew women are not as the Egyptian women; for they are lively, and are delivered ere the midwives come in unto them" (Exodus 1:17–19).

We need not assume that Puah and Shiprah lied to Pharaoh. Hebrew women were hardworking and may indeed have been of a physical constitution that tended toward quicker deliveries than the more leisurely Egyptian aristocrats. But whether or not their story to Pharaoh was entirely true, they valued the innocent lives of the babies Pharaoh would have killed. The courage required to do the right thing in the face of grave danger was a holy thing that pleased God.

"Therefore God dealt well with the midwives: and the people multiplied, and waxed very mighty. And it came to pass, because the midwives feared God, that he made them houses" (Exodus 1:20–21).

What a happy example of "what goes around comes around"! At some point, Puah and Shiprah both realized that they themselves were also with child. The pregnancies resulted in live, healthy babies, as God's special blessing rested on these women for the choices they made. If they had boys, what must have run through Puah's and Shiprah's minds when those newborn males cried for the first time?

God's Word is replete with affirmations of the holiness of valuing human life.

"Whoso sheddeth man's blood, by man shall his blood be shed: for in the image of God made he man" (Genesis 9:6).

This verse comes from the covenant that God made with Noah, long before Abraham, the children of Israel, or the Ten Commandments.

"The innocent and righteous slay thou not: for I will not justify the wicked" (Exodus 23:7).

God tells Moses here that innocent human life must not be taken and that God is the fearsome judge of those who break this cardinal law.

King Solomon, the wisest man who ever lived, included lack of respect for human life in the top seven things that God hates most.

"These six things doth the Lord hate: yea, seven are an abomination unto him: A proud look, a lying tongue, and hands that shed innocent blood, An heart that deviseth wicked imaginations, feet that be swift in running to mischief, A false witness that speaketh lies, and he that soweth discord among brethren" (Proverbs 6:16–19).

Both Ezekiel and Job give a reason, beyond the obvious, about why respect for human life is a holy choice:

"Behold, all souls are mine; as the soul of the father, so also the soul of the son is mine" (Ezekiel 18:4a).

"In whose hand is the soul of every living thing, and the breath of all mankind" (Job 12:10).

Taking the life of another is stealing something that does not belong to the killer—one of God's created souls.

But enough about the immorality of traditionally defined murder. While we're on the subject of babies, is there any biblical basis to go a step further and extend this prohibition against taking human life to a prohibition against taking the life of an unborn child?

When God called young, reluctant Jeremiah to be a prophet, he said something very interesting: "Then the word of the Lord came unto me, saying, *Before I formed thee in the belly I knew thee*; and before thou camest forth out of the womb I sanctified thee, and I ordained thee a prophet unto the nations" (Jeremiah 1:4–5, emphasis added).

Apparently God wasn't waiting around to see if the mother was willing to carry her child to term. He had plans for Jeremiah that went back to before his conception! Jeremiah was in God's hands during his fetal development and was destined to deliver God's message before he was even old enough to make the choice to serve Him.

One of the most famous Scriptures used to make a case for the personhood of the unborn can be found in a song that King David wrote.

"For thou hast possessed my reins: *thou hast covered me in my mother's womb*. I will praise thee; for I am fearfully and wonderfully made: marvellous are thy works; and that my soul knoweth right well. My substance was not hid from thee, when I was made in secret, and curiously wrought in the lowest parts of the earth. *Thine eyes did see my substance, yet being unperfect*; and in thy book all my members were written, which in continuance were fashioned, when as yet there was none of them" (Psalm 139:13–16, emphasis added).

Does it really make sense for us to believe, on the one hand, that God valued the lives of the baby boys who were born to Hebrew women and in danger of Pharaoh's sword but then not believe that God also valued those same lives the day before, when they were still in the womb? Or the week before? Or the month before? In other words, at what point during fetal development is it too soon for God to cherish the growing baby?

God spoke to another prophet about his interest in and concern for the unborn.

"Thus saith the Lord that made thee, *and formed thee from the womb*, which will help thee; Fear not, O Jacob, my servant; and thou, Jesurun, whom I have chosen. … Thus saith the Lord, thy redeemer, *and he that formed thee from the womb*, I am the Lord that maketh all things; that stretcheth forth the heavens alone; that spreadeth abroad the earth by myself" (Isaiah 44:2, 24, emphasis added).

If God is the Creator, then fetal development is much, much more than a biological process of cell division. To interrupt it would be to interfere with God's very plan for the life of another human being. Should we not respect each little life from the moment that it is conceived?

There's another undervalued time of life that God's Word calls us to respect and protect—grave sickness and old age.

"Then said his wife unto him, Dost thou still retain thine integrity? curse God, and die. But he said unto her, Thou speakest as one of the foolish women speaketh. What? shall we receive good at the hand of God, and shall we not receive evil? In all this did not Job sin with his lips" (Job 2:9–10).

Job lost everything he had, and then God allowed Satan to make him terribly ill. His wife seems to be urging him to commit suicide here—an act some would probably label justifiable or an act of euthanasia. But even in his darkest hour, Job recognizes the great value of the life God had given him, and he would have none of it.

But wait a minute. My life is my own. Even if we accept the premise that no one has the right to take the life of another human, including an unborn one, can we not at least grant each person the right to decide for himself whether he will go on living?

"Know ye not that ye are the temple of God, and that the Spirit of God dwelleth in you? If any man defile the temple of God, him shall God destroy; for the temple of God is holy, which temple ye are" (1 Corinthians 3:16–17).

Paul doesn't build a lot of wiggle room into this Scripture. He summarily condemns anyone who would take his own life. We know that God is merciful, and some people are not in a rational state when they make such decisions. We cannot say how God would judge any one individual, and we should never use a verse like this to heap pain on the family of someone who has committed suicide. But at the very least, the text is clear that God does not grant to any person the right to take his own life.

Later in that very same letter to the Corinthians, Paul describes death as a bad thing, rather than something to be looked forward to or to embrace:

"The last enemy that shall be destroyed is death" (1 Corinthians 15:26).

Of course, the Christian can experience victory, even in death, and the hope of the saints for life beyond the grave is a wonderful thing. But death came into the world in the first place as the result of man's sin, and it is no friend to the human race. In other words, the take-home message is simply that God greatly values life, and people should too.

The holiness of a respect for life must go beyond merely making sure that you don't ever kill anyone. It extends to being a hero for those who are in danger of death at the hands of someone else:

"If thou forbear to deliver them that are drawn unto death, and those that are ready to be slain; If thou sayest, Behold, we knew it not; doth not he that pondereth the heart consider it? and he that keepeth thy soul, doth not he know it? and shall not he render to every man according to his works?" (Proverbs 24:11–12, emphasis added).

God was well pleased with the holy choices that Puah and Shiprah made, when they could have acted in fear to save their own skins instead. Would he not also be pleased by the efforts of his followers to promote pro-life values and respect for the lives of the elderly and sick? We dare not indulge in the luxury of turning our heads and doing nothing. Human life is too precious. Let us make the holy choice to protect and preserve it at every available opportunity.

CHAPTER 5

Moses Responds with Meekness

The date is about 1461 BC. God called Abraham over five hundred years ago. Now, eighty-one-year-old Moses is in the wilderness with the children Israel, on the way back to the Promised Land in Canaan after centuries in Egypt. God delivered the people from their slavery there about a year and a half ago. Then he provided daily manna from heaven for food, and water gushed from a rock for the thirsty throngs. It was just last year that God's Law was given to Moses on Mount Sinai and only about six months ago that the tent tabernacle, containing the ark of the covenant was finished, according to the plans given in the Law. A priesthood has been established through the lineage of Moses's brother Aaron too.

> Now Korah, the son of Izhar, the son of Kohath, the son of Levi, and Dathan and Abiram, the sons of Eliab, and On, the son of Peleth, sons of Reuben, took men: And they rose up before Moses, with certain

of the children of Israel, two hundred and fifty princes of the assembly, famous in the congregation, men of renown: And they gathered themselves together against Moses and against Aaron, and said unto them, Ye take too much upon you, seeing all the congregation are holy, every one of them, and the Lord is among them: wherefore then lift ye up yourselves above the congregation of the Lord? And when Moses heard it, he fell upon his face: And he spake unto Korah and unto all his company, saying, Even to morrow the Lord will shew who are his, and who is holy; and will cause him to come near unto him: even him whom he hath chosen will he cause to come near unto him. This do; Take you censers, Korah, and all his company; And put fire therein, and put incense in them before the Lord to morrow: and it shall be that the man whom the Lord doth choose, he shall be holy: ye take too much upon you, ye sons of Levi. And Moses said unto Korah, Hear, I pray you, ye sons of Levi: Seemeth it but a small thing unto you, that the God of Israel hath separated you from the congregation of Israel, to bring you near to himself to do the service of the tabernacle of the Lord, and to stand before the congregation to minister unto them? And he hath brought thee near to him, and all thy brethren the sons of Levi with thee: and seek ye the priesthood also? For which cause both thou and all thy company are gathered together against the Lord: and what is Aaron, that ye murmur against him? And Moses sent to call Dathan and Abiram, the sons of Eliab: which said, We will not come up: Is it a small thing that thou hast brought us up out of a land that floweth with milk and honey, to kill us in the wilderness, except thou make thyself altogether a prince over us? Moreover thou hast not brought us into a land that floweth with milk and honey, or given us inheritance of fields and vineyards: wilt thou put out the eyes of these men? we will not come up. And Moses was very wroth, and said unto the Lord, Respect not thou their offering: I have not taken one ass from them, neither have I hurt one of them. And Moses said unto Korah, Be thou and all thy company before the Lord, thou, and they, and Aaron, to morrow: And take every man his censer, and put incense in them, and bring ye before the Lord every man his censer, two hundred and fifty censers; thou also, and Aaron, each of you his censer. And they took every man his censer, and put fire in them, and laid incense thereon, and stood in the door of the tabernacle of the congregation with Moses and Aaron. And Korah gathered all the congregation against them unto the door of the tabernacle of the congregation: and the glory of the Lord appeared unto all the congregation. And the Lord spake unto Moses and unto Aaron, saying, Separate yourselves from among this congregation, that I may consume them in a moment. And they fell upon their faces, and said, O God, the God of the spirits of all flesh, shall one man sin, and wilt thou be wroth with all the congregation? And the Lord spake unto Moses, saying, Speak unto the congregation, saying, Get you up from about the tabernacle of Korah, Dathan, and Abiram. And Moses rose up and went unto Dathan and Abiram; and the elders of Israel followed him. And he spake unto the congregation, saying, Depart, I pray you, from the tents of these wicked men, and touch nothing of theirs, lest ye be consumed in all their sins. So they gat up from the tabernacle of Korah, Dathan, and Abiram, on every side: and Dathan and Abiram came out, and stood in the door of their tents, and their wives, and their sons, and their little children. And Moses said, Hereby ye shall know that the Lord hath sent me to do all these works; for I have not done them of mine own mind. If these men die the common death of all men, or if they be visited after the visitation of all men; then the Lord hath not sent me. But if the Lord make a new thing, and the earth open her mouth, and swallow them up, with all that appertain unto them, and they go down quick into the pit; then ye shall understand that these men have provoked the Lord. And it came to pass, as he had made an end of speaking all these words, that the ground clave asunder that was under them: And the earth opened her mouth, and swallowed them up, and their houses, and all the men that appertained unto Korah, and all their goods. They, and all that appertained to them, went down alive into the pit, and the earth closed upon them: and they perished from among the congregation. And all Israel that were round about them fled at the cry of them: for they said, Lest the earth swallow us up also. And there came out a fire from the Lord, and consumed the two hundred and fifty men that offered incense. And the Lord spake unto Moses, saying, Speak unto Eleazar the son of Aaron the priest, that he take up the censers out of the burning, and scatter thou the fire yonder; for they are hallowed. The censers of these sinners against their own souls, let them make them broad plates for a covering of the altar: for they offered them before the Lord, therefore they are hallowed: and they shall be a sign unto the children of Israel. And Eleazar the priest took the brasen censers, wherewith they that were burnt had offered; and they were made broad plates for a covering of the altar: To be a memorial unto the children of Israel, that no stranger, which is not of the seed of Aaron, come near to offer incense before the Lord; that he be not as Korah, and as his company: as the Lord said to him by the hand of Moses. But on the morrow all the congregation of the children of Israel murmured against Moses and against Aaron, saying, Ye have killed the people of the Lord. And it came to pass, when the congregation was gathered against Moses and against Aaron, that they looked toward the tabernacle of the congregation: and, behold, the cloud covered it, and the glory of the Lord appeared. And Moses and Aaron came before the tabernacle of the congregation. And the Lord spake unto Moses, saying, Get you up from among this congregation, that I may consume them as in a moment. And they fell upon their faces. And Moses said unto Aaron, Take a censer, and put fire therein from off the altar, and put on incense, and go quickly unto the congregation, and make an atonement for them: for there is wrath gone out from the Lord; the plague is begun. And Aaron took as Moses commanded, and ran into the midst of the congregation; and, behold, the plague was begun among the people: and he put on incense, and made an atonement for the people. And he stood between the dead and the living; and the plague was stayed. Now they that died in the plague were fourteen thousand and seven hundred, beside them that died about the matter of Korah. And Aaron returned unto Moses unto the door of the tabernacle of the congregation: and the plague was stayed. (Numbers 16:1–50)

Recorded in this same book of Numbers, just a few chapters before the story, is an amazing claim about Moses: "(Now the man Moses was very meek, above all the men which were upon the face of the earth.)" (Numbers 12:3).

It seems strange that the humblest man alive should be chided by his followers for being arrogant. False accusations can be enraging, and the things that Korah and his men said against Moses *did* seem to upset him greatly, as they should have. But Moses's amazingly humble response had five beautiful facets to it that were well pleasing to the Lord.

1. Bowed Down to the Ground

Moses was caught off guard by Korah's attack, to say the least. He didn't have a lot of time to formulate a response or to compose himself. He appears to have reacted on pure instinct, which was to assume the humblest posture of all—to bow down. What an awesome indication of the character of Moses and the integrity of his heart! Then, as the story progressed and God threatened twice to wipe out the people, Moses bowed himself to the ground again on both of those occasions. A lesser man might have stood there, arms folded, with a defiant look of victory on his face as he watched God wreak destruction on the crowd. But Moses did not dare to elevate himself before anyone, even after being made the leader of a nation by God himself.

Body language speaks volumes, and if you really mean to convey meekness, you can intuitively do so by how you position yourself.

Even though not every situation today calls for bowing down to the ground, humble, open posture is still an appropriate way to defuse another person's accusations in a family, in a workplace, or in a neighborhood. Facial expressions can be hard and angry, or they can be soft and kind. Arms can be crossed or hands can be on hips, conveying indignation and anger, or fists can be unclenched and arms outstretched. Head can be back, with nose in the air, or eyes can be downcast. Body language speaks volumes, and if you really mean to convey meekness, you can intuitively do so by how you position yourself.

"Humble yourselves in the sight of the Lord, and he shall lift you up" (James 4:10).

"Who are kept by the power of God through faith unto salvation ready to be revealed in the last time. Wherein ye greatly rejoice, though now for a season, if need be, ye are in heaviness through manifold temptations" (1 Peter 5:5–6).

2. Refused to Take the Insult Personally

Insults make most people pretty defensive. A typical reaction is to think along the lines of "How *dare* you?" Moses *was* mortified that Korah and his men dared to accuse him of lording it over them, but he knew that their sin was a reflection on them, rather than on anything he or Aaron had done. Note his response: "For which cause both thou and all thy company are gathered together against the Lord: and what is Aaron, that ye murmur against him?" (Numbers 16:11).

Learning not to take an insult personally is one of the best ways to avoid losing your temper. Imagine confronting a hostile driver in heavy traffic. Maybe some guy pulls out in front of you, cutting you off, and to add to the rudeness of it all, he turns around, makes eye contact with you, and then flashes an obscene gesture. Wouldn't you feel incensed and as though you'd really been done wrong? But before reacting in a foolish way, think for a second. That driver doesn't know you, and he likely would have done the same thing to someone else who happened to be in the position in which you found yourself on that road. It's not about you. It's about him. Take a deep breath, and let his actions reflect on his character, not yours. That's how Moses preserved his sanity!

"Blessed are ye, when men shall revile you, and persecute you, and shall say all manner of evil against you falsely, for my sake" (Matthew 5:11).

Jesus is teaching here that other people's abuse against you for the sake of His kingdom is not about you. You're not to blame; rather, you're to be rewarded! He says that persecution is nothing new, because even the Old Testament prophets endured it. See it for what it is, and move on, praising the Lord all the while.

3. Took His Frustrations to God

Moses could have fussed and fumed at the people, or he could have railed on the perpetrators. He could have gone home to his wife and ranted about them in private, or he could have gossiped about them to his brother Aaron and sister Miriam. Instead, he prayed.

"And Moses was very wroth, and said unto the Lord, Respect not thou their offering: I have not taken one ass from them, neither have I hurt one of them" (Numbers 16:15).

Moses was indignant, and he had good reason to be. But he spoke about it to the Lord and asked Him to take care of it. King David did the same thing, even turning his prayer into a song.

"Plead my cause, O Lord, with them that strive with me: fight against them that fight against me. Take hold of shield and buckler, and stand up for mine help. Draw out also the spear, and stop the way against them that persecute me: say unto my soul, I am thy salvation. Let them be confounded and put to shame that seek after my soul: let them be turned back and brought to confusion that devise my hurt" (Psalm 35:1–4).

Where do you turn when you're attacked? Do you long to hash it over with anyone who will listen? Do you get on the phone, or begin an email campaign, or dissect it over lunch with a good friend? That's not where God wants you to take your concerns. Take them to him. He is just, and he will hear.

4. Interceded for the People

"And they fell upon their faces, and said, O God, the God of the spirits of all flesh, shall one man sin, and wilt thou be wroth with all the congregation?" (Numbers 16:22).

Moses prayed for the sheep-like people who were nodding their heads and amen-ing the troublemakers. You'd think he'd be hoping for their destruction, but he *prayed* for them! What a merciful and godly man he was! No wonder the Torah prophesied that the Messiah would be "like unto Moses." What a holy and acceptable choice he made in this situation.

> But I say unto you, Love your enemies, bless them that curse you, do good to them that hate you, and pray for them which despitefully use you, and persecute you; That ye may be the children of your Father which is in heaven: for he maketh his sun to rise on the evil and on the good, and sendeth rain on the just and on the unjust. For if ye love them which love you, what reward have ye? do not even the publicans the same? And if ye salute your brethren only, what do ye more than others? do not even the publicans so? Be ye therefore perfect, even as your Father which is in heaven is perfect. (Matthew 5:44–48)

Jesus's Sermon on the Mount goes along exactly with Moses's choices in his trials with the Israelites. He seems to have been a man ahead of his time.

Got something against someone at the moment? Have you prayed for him or her? Have you tried to see that person through the eyes of a God who created and loved him and wants the best for him? Interceding for others might change you as much as it changes them.

5. Made Atonement for Their Sins

"And Moses said unto Aaron, Take a censer, and put fire therein from off the altar, and put on incense, and go quickly unto the congregation, and make an atonement for them: for there is wrath gone out from the Lord; the plague is begun" (Numbers 16:46).

Foreshadowing the atonement of Christ, Moses urged his brother Aaron to act in the office of priest to offer fire from the altar to God, that the people's sin in following Korah might be forgiven. He didn't want to see the plague wipe them out, even though that fate would have been perfectly just. Moses felt compassion, so he showed mercy. I wonder how it felt when the people realized that the only reason some of them were still alive was that the very man they had gone against had gone to God on their behalf.

You don't have to offer atonement to God for anyone today, but you can act in a similar fashion by making peace between people or urging them to make peace with God whenever you have the chance.

"Blessed are the peacemakers: for they shall be called the children of God" (Matthew 5:9).

Moses faced a very difficult test, and he earned an A++. You can be sure that your pride will be tested too. You'll be misunderstood, or accused, or treated unfairly, or railed on without cause. Will you react with holy humility?

As an aside and as a sharp contrast to Moses's sterling behavior, note that Korah made the New Testament "Hall of Infamy" in the book of Jude for his arrogance.

> Beloved, when I gave all diligence to write unto you of the common salvation, it was needful for me to write unto you, and exhort you that ye should earnestly contend for the faith which was once delivered unto

the saints. ... For there are certain men crept in unawares, who were before of old ordained to this condemnation, ungodly men, turning the grace of our God into lasciviousness, and denying the only Lord God, and our Lord Jesus Christ. ... Woe unto them! for they have gone in the way of Cain, and ran greedily after the error of Balaam for reward, *and perished in the gainsaying of Core.* (Jude 1:1, 4, 11, emphasis added)

Just as Korah denied the divinely appointed leadership of Moses, godless men today deny the lordship of Jesus Christ. To say "I haven't done anything wrong, and I don't need a Savior" is to be in arrogant rebellion. And rejecting Christ is the most unholy act of all.

Bottom line: the story of Korah and Moses enjoins us to put on beautiful holiness by humbling ourselves before God and others. Is your heart bowed before God?

CHAPTER 6

Ruth Cares for Her Widowed Mother-in-Law

After Moses brought the people to the edge of the Promised Land, he bequeathed his position of leadership to his mentor, Joshua, and then he died. Joshua helped the nation conquer the wicked, idolatrous peoples living in Canaan. After Joshua's death, Israel began a period of about four hundred years in which their rulers were judges, as though the chief justice of the Supreme Court was the head of the government. These judges were periodically raised up by God to nudge a backslidden people to return to obeying the Law, but when they died, sin came to the fore again.

About 146 years or so into the "age of the judges," famine came to small town known as Bethlehem, or "House of Bread." A Bethlehemite named Elimelech and his wife decided that times were just too hard there, so they asked around and heard that back east, in the land of Moab, people had plenty to eat. Moab was the last place the Israelites stopped before they came to their Promised Land and was the burial place of Moses (Deuteronomy 34:4–8). The Moabites were descendents of the incestuous relationship of Abraham's nephew Lot with his very own daughter (Genesis 19:36–38), and Moabites worshiped idols. But at least they weren't hungry at that time, so Elimelech and Naomi took their boys and hit the road.

While they were there in Moab, the sons married local women. Then tragedy came to the family. One by one, all three men died—first Elimelech himself and then his two sons. The Bible doesn't say how they passed away, but Naomi's life was filled with grief that only an unfortunate few today can imagine.

By this time the famine in Bethlehem had subsided, and Naomi had some critical decisions to make about how to support herself and her daughters-in-law in the future. She packed them up and planned to return home, when it struck her that perhaps the girls would be better off remaining in their home country. After all, Jewish Law would make it difficult for a Moabite widow to have any kind of future in Israel:

> An Ammonite or Moabite shall not enter into the congregation of the Lord; even to their tenth generation shall they not enter into the congregation of the Lord for ever: Because they met you not with bread and with water in the way, when ye came forth out of Egypt; and because they hired against thee Balaam the son of Beor of Pethor of Mesopotamia, to curse thee. Nevertheless the Lord thy God would not hearken unto Balaam; but the Lord thy God turned the curse into a blessing unto thee, because the Lord thy God loved thee. Thou shalt not seek their peace nor their prosperity all thy days for ever. (Deuteronomy 23:3–6)

Whether Naomi mentioned the reception the widows might expect back in Judah is not divulged. However, she overcame any selfish impulse to keep her daughters-in-law with her for the sake of companionship and urged them to turn around and head for their parents' homes.

"And Naomi said unto her two daughters in law, Go, return each to her mother's house: the Lord deal kindly with you, as ye have dealt with the dead, and with me. The Lord grant you that ye may find rest, each of you in the house of her husband. Then she kissed them; and they lifted up their voice, and wept. And they said unto her, Surely we will return with thee unto thy people" (Ruth 1:8–10).

Naomi must have been quite a woman. These girls preferred to live with her, even after their husbands were dead, rather than return to their people, culture, and birth families. She must have treated them with great kindness and respect. Her investment in the relationship had sure netted their return affection for her.

> And Naomi said, Turn again, my daughters: why will ye go with me? are there yet any more sons in my womb, that they may be your husbands? Turn again, my daughters, go your way; for I am too old to have an husband. If I should say, I have hope, if I should have an husband also to night, and should also bear sons; Would ye tarry for them till they were grown? would ye stay for them from having husbands? nay, my daughters; for it grieveth me much for your sakes that the hand of the Lord is gone out against me. (Ruth 1:11–13)

Naomi didn't have much prospect for a happy future back home, but she'd rather forgo the companionship of her beloved daughters-in-law than subject them to a future without marriage and children, like the one she now faced. But one of the daughters-in-law was having nothing of it:

"And Ruth said, Intreat me not to leave thee, or to return from following after thee: for whither thou goest, I will go; and where thou lodgest, I will lodge: thy people shall be my people, and thy God my God: Where thou diest, will I die, and there will I be buried: the Lord do so to me, and more also, if ought but death part thee and me. When she saw that she was stedfastly minded to go with her, then she left speaking unto her" (Ruth 1:16–18).

Ruth loved Naomi so much that she refused to live without her. Ruth put her foot down and stated once and forever her intentions to stay with Naomi for the rest of her life. This famous decree of fidelity is so absolute that it makes a lovely reading at weddings. It's often the page to which the Bible is turned as a backdrop for a wedding photo of a couple's hands wearing their rings.

Back in Bethlehem, Naomi was none too chipper. As she encountered people she hadn't seen in years, her response to their greetings was depressing.

"So they two went until they came to Bethlehem. And it came to pass, when they were come to Bethlehem, that all the city was moved about them, and they said, Is this Naomi? And she said unto them, Call me not Naomi, call me Mara: for the Almighty hath dealt very bitterly with me. I went out full and the Lord hath brought me home again empty: why then call ye me Naomi, seeing the Lord hath testified against me, and the Almighty hath afflicted me?" (Ruth 1:19–21).

Ruth took the situation in stride, though, and began to think practically. Since Jewish Law allowed the poor to go behind reapers and take what they had missed or dropped, Ruth immediately employed herself in this low-wage and demeaning job, so she could put food on the table for her "mom."

"And Ruth the Moabitess said unto Naomi, Let me now go to the field, and glean ears of corn after him in whose sight I shall find grace. And she said unto her, Go, my daughter. And she went, and came, and gleaned in the field after the reapers: and her hap was to light on a part of the field belonging unto Boaz, who was of the kindred of Elimelech" (Ruth 2:2–3).

Like the wording there? "And her hap was to light on a part..." In other words, "As it turned out, she found herself ..." The Lord left nothing to chance for this faithful and godly Moabite-turned-Israelite convert. God did allow her beloved husband to pass away, and that was hard to understand, but he hadn't abandoned her, and he had a plan.

"Then said Boaz unto Ruth, Hearest thou not, my daughter? Go not to glean in another field, neither go from hence, but abide here fast by my maidens: Let thine eyes be on the field that they do reap, and go thou after them: have I not charged the young men that they shall not touch thee? and when thou art athirst, go unto the vessels, and drink of that which the young men have drawn" (Ruth 2:8–9).

The rich boss of the land in this hostile-to-Moabites country pronounced a blessing on hard-working Ruth. Perhaps even he didn't realize that he spoke in the office of a prophet when he said those words. Ruth was to be blessed indeed.

As the days went by and Ruth kept the wolf from the door of her home by working as a farm laborer, Naomi again showed her concern for her "adopted daughter." In fact, she came up with a plan that resulted in Ruth's engagement to her single, wealthy boss who was, by chance, a part of Naomi's extended family by marriage!

> Then Naomi her mother in law said unto her, My daughter, shall I not seek rest for thee, that it may be well with thee? And now is not Boaz of our kindred, with whose maidens thou wast? Behold, he winnoweth barley to night in the threshingfloor. Wash thyself therefore, and anoint thee, and put thy raiment upon thee, and get thee down to the floor: but make not thyself known unto the man, until he

shall have done eating and drinking. And it shall be, when he lieth down, that thou shalt mark the place where he shall lie, and thou shalt go in, and uncover his feet, and lay thee down; and he will tell thee what thou shalt do. And she said unto her, All that thou sayest unto me I will do. And she went down unto the floor, and did according to all that her mother in law bade her ... And he said, Blessed be thou of the Lord, my daughter: for thou hast shewed more kindness in the latter end than at the beginning, inasmuch as thou followedst not young men, whether poor or rich. And now, my daughter, fear not; I will do to thee all that thou requirest: for all the city of my people doth know that thou art a virtuous woman. (Ruth 3:1–6, 10–11)

Ruth was gutsy to follow through in obedience to the suggestions Naomi made, but everything paid off when Boaz agreed to marry her. The result was a happily-ever-after ending that even superseded a fairy tale:

And all the people that were in the gate, and the elders, said, We are witnesses. The Lord make the woman that is come into thine house like Rachel and like Leah, which two did build the house of Israel: and do thou worthily in Ephratah, and be famous in Bethlehem: And let thy house be like the house of Pharez, whom Tamar bare unto Judah, of the seed which the Lord shall give thee of this young woman. So Boaz took Ruth, and she was his wife: and when he went in unto her, the Lord gave her conception, and she bare a son. And the women said unto Naomi, Blessed be the Lord, which hath not left thee this day without a kinsman, that his name may be famous in Israel. And he shall be unto thee a restorer of thy life, and a nourisher of thine old age: for thy daughter in law, which loveth thee, which is better to thee than seven sons, hath born him. And Naomi took the child, and laid it in her bosom, and became nurse unto it. And the women her neighbours gave it a name, saying, There is a son born to Naomi; and they called his name Obed: he is the father of Jesse, the father of David. (Ruth 4:11–17)

Not even the most generous prediction could have placed this Moabite woman in the genealogy of the Messiah himself! Not only is Ruth listed as the great-grandmother of King David in the Old Testament, but the gospel of Matthew specifically mentions her as an ancestor of Jesus Christ.

The book of the generation of Jesus Christ, the son of David, the son of Abraham. Abraham begat Isaac; and Isaac begat Jacob; and Jacob begat Judas and his brethren; And Judas begat Phares and Zara of Thamar; and Phares begat Esrom; and Esrom begat Aram; And Aram begat Aminadab; and Aminadab begat Naasson; and Naasson begat Salmon; And Salmon begat Booz of Rachab; and Booz begat Obed of Ruth; and Obed begat

Jesse; And Jesse begat David the king; and David the king begat Solomon of her that had been the wife of Urias. (Matthew 1:1–6)

Ruth's commitment was such an act of holiness that it stands to inspire Christians now.

Ruth's commitment was such an act of holiness that it stands to inspire Christians now. Both her words and her deeds demonstrated without contradiction that she was with Naomi for the long haul. And when life calls for commitment today—in a marriage, in a parent/

child relationship, in the body of Christ, or in a friendship—that same spirit of complete commitment will set you up for a harvest of blessing.

Ruth's Words

Ruth's famous and simple verbal affirmation to Naomi contains seven statements of commitment:

1. Never leave you
2. Go with you
3. Stay with you
4. Embrace your people
5. Embrace your God
6. Die where you die
7. Be buried where you are buried

If you want to be a part of the people of God today, the body of Christ, you'll need each of these seven parts of commitment as you walk with Him. Tell Him in prayer that (1) you will not forsake your faith, (2) you will go where He leads, (3) you will stay with Him through thick and thin, (4) you will embrace other Christians, even when they aren't so easy to love, (5) you will embrace Him as Lord of your life, (6) you'll carry your commitment to your deathbed, and (7) you'll trust your soul to Him beyond the grave.

Words are powerful, and they can really change things. If you've been on the fence as a Christian, sort of sampling a walk of faith without really getting in all the way, let this be the day of new beginnings. Make your commitment to Christ a total one, *not just in heart but in words.* Use Ruth's example as a template, and tell the Lord you're always going to be His. It will change your life forever.

Ruth's Actions

After Ruth told Naomi what her intentions were for the future, she backed it up with three main deeds.

First, Ruth forsook all others. That wasn't always real pleasant either. When she arrived in Bethlehem, she was a foreigner from an idolatrous land. She didn't know a soul except Naomi, and her future presumably was bleak. But Ruth plugged ahead because she had on blinders. Her life was with Naomi, and that was final.

The Christian should approach a walk with Jesus in the same way. It is such a blessed privilege to stay with Him that it simply doesn't matter if the world sees us as strange or stigmatized. It doesn't matter if those around us don't have much in common with us or if they think our lives hold little hope of fun or fulfillment. We just plug ahead, and we put on blinders. Eternity with Christ is our destiny, and we're moving toward our beloved.

Second, Ruth worked hard to provide for her mother-in-law. She didn't expect her commitment to Naomi to afford her ease or luxury, even though it eventually did just that. She got up in the morning and braced herself for a lot of backbreaking effort.

There was nothing lazy about Ruth, and there can be nothing lazy about Christ's committed followers now. Living for him necessarily means working for him. You don't have the luxury of deciding whether or not to get involved in the local church. As a part of the bride of Jesus, you simply must. Find a place where you can work, roll up your sleeves, and get after it. Make a real effort, and expect to keep going. You're not His just to sit around and soak up resources. He'll provide, but He expects you to do your part.

Third, Ruth trusted Naomi so much that she submitted to her in complete obedience, even when it put her out of a safe comfort zone. Going to the threshing floor to sneak up on her rich boss in the middle of the night must have been terrifying! What would people think she was doing if they saw? What if Naomi was all wrong about the possibility of a marriage? What if Boaz yelled at her and banned her from gleaning in his fields after that? But Ruth's love for and commitment to Naomi extended to confidence in Naomi's judgment and ability to steer their future together. Just as she had trusted Naomi to resettle the two of them in Bethlehem, she trusted her now to direct actions that were bold and out of the box.

Can you trust the one to whom you've committed? Let me reassure you that God *can* be trusted. When things aren't going right in your life, he can be trusted to get you through, stand by you, comfort you, give you wisdom, and bring something good out of it. Trust him, submit to his wishes, take a risk, and humble yourself before him.

- If he lays it on your heart to fast, trust him, and do it.
- If he lays it on your heart to witness to someone, trust him, and do it.
- If he lays it on your heart to apologize or make peace with someone, trust him, and do it.

Get the point? Take a risk, humble yourself, and submit.

Ruth's holy choices could not have paid off bigger. You'll find the same to be true in your own life. You may not marry a rich spouse, and you won't become an ancestor of the Messiah. But if you will make a complete commitment to Christ and follow through for the rest of your life, you will be brought to a place where God can so bless you that you may not have room to receive it.

CHAPTER 7

David Pours out the Gift of Water

After four hundred years of being ruled by judges, Israel insisted on a king, and God reluctantly granted them one in the form of Saul, a tall, shy man from the tribe of Benjamin. Saul started out well, and God allowed him to reign for forty fairly stable years, but he disobeyed on several key occasions. God sent the prophet Samuel to announce to Saul that the possibility of a dynasty was being taken away from his family. Saul's son Jonathan would never be king. Saul appears to have descended into mental illness after that, and he finally committed suicide in battle after an enemy wounded him.

God's choice for the second king of Israel was Ruth's great-grandson David, who was born in Ruth's adopted town of Bethlehem. David was the eighth of eight boys, and he began his adult life as a shepherd. After his unlikely victory as a teenager over the giant Philistine Goliath, his musicianship won him a job playing harp and singing for King Saul, who was becoming temperamental and mentally unstable. Eventually, Saul's envy of

David made it necessary for David to run for his life. After years of living on the lam, David came out of hiding when Saul died in battle. David was then made king over his own tribe of Judah, while a son of Saul reigned over the rest of Israel for a couple of years. Finally, Saul's son was killed by two of his own captains, and David ruled over all Israel.

Second Samuel 5:17 begins a story that took place about 1017 BC. By that time, David had been king for about seven years, and he had just moved the capital from the city of Hebron to Jerusalem. His perennial enemies, the Philistines, were after him again, and he'd fled from Jerusalem, asked the Lord for direction, and later attacked the Philistines on their own turf, achieving a victory. Unfortunately, the Philistines didn't stay down too long. Finis Dake speculated in his Bible commentary that it was probably about the time of the barley harvest in April, because kings often went to war in spring after the early rains.

> And the Philistines came up yet again, and spread themselves in the valley of Rephaim. And when David enquired of the Lord, he said, Thou shalt not go up; but fetch a compass behind them, and come upon them over against the mulberry trees. And let it be, when thou hearest the sound of a going in the tops of the mulberry trees, that then thou shalt bestir thyself: for then shall the Lord go out before thee, to smite the host of the Philistines. And David did so, as the Lord had commanded him; and smote the Philistines from Geba until thou come to Gazer. (2 Samuel 5:22–25)

Winning a battle is not always an instantaneous thing, and sometimes the enemy gains ground before he is conquered. King David found himself camping in a cave in none-too-pleasant conditions:

"And three of the thirty chief went down, and came to David in the harvest time unto the cave of Adullam: and the troop of the Philistines pitched in the valley of Rephaim. And David was then in an hold, and the garrison of the Philistines was then in Bethlehem. And David longed, and said, Oh that one would give me drink of the water of the well of Bethlehem, which is by the gate!" (2 Samuel 23:13–15).

Have you ever ardently longed for something comforting that was just out of reach? A piece of chocolate, a comfortable bed, a chance to talk to someone you love who is far away, or even just a warm bubble bath can create indescribable desire when it simply cannot be had. King David was used to the wonderful water from Jerusalem. Perhaps the water in the cave where he was staying tasted odd because it was full of minerals. Perhaps the cave was dry, so his men had to collect water from a muddy stream or pond. In any case, all David wanted was a drink to quench his thirst, and what was available just wasn't cutting it.

"And the three mighty men brake through the host of the Philistines, and drew water out of the well of Bethlehem, that was by the gate, and took it, and brought it to David: nevertheless he would not drink thereof, but poured it out unto the Lord. And he said, Be it far from me, O Lord, that I should do this: is not this the blood of the men that went in jeopardy of their lives? therefore he would not drink it. These things did these three mighty men" (2 Samuel 23:16–17).

Can you believe what you're reading? *He wouldn't drink it! He poured it out!* Can you hear it splashing on the hard floor of the cave? His willingness to make this holy sacrifice to God and control an urge to consume it in a frenzy is surely one of the most awe-inspiring passages in Scripture.

What could such a story possibly mean to people who live thousands of years later and have plenty of good-tasting water to drink? David demonstrated three key characteristics of holiness that are timeless examples to people everywhere who would like to draw nearer to God.

1. Discern the Sacred

"Is not this the blood of the men that went in jeopardy of their lives?" (2 Samuel 23:17).

This act of devotion by three of David's proven and mightiest men delighted the heart of David, and he saw in it a sacrifice of which the Lord alone is worthy. Perhaps when David recognized the great risk his men took in providing him with his favorite water to drink, he thought of something in the Torah:

> And whatsoever man there be of the house of Israel, or of the strangers that sojourn among you, that eateth any manner of blood; I will even set my face against that soul that eateth blood, and will cut him off from among his people. For the life of the flesh is in the blood: and I have given it to you upon the altar to make an atonement for your souls: for it is the blood that maketh an atonement for the soul. Therefore I said unto the children of Israel, No soul of you shall eat blood, neither shall any stranger that sojourneth among you eat blood. (Leviticus 17:10–12)

David saw the water as the very blood of the men who'd gone to get it. Hence, he refused to drink their "blood" and poured it out before the Lord.

Something sacred is special, set apart, devoted, or designated to God. What in your life needs to be set apart as sacred? How about life itself, sex, the Lord's Day, your tithe, time alone with God, His precious Word, or the ministry He has called you to. Let me explain:

- If you recognize that sex is sacred, you won't be so inclined to laugh at a dirty joke, or look at porn, or sleep around.

- If you recognize that life is sacred, you won't be so inclined to believe that sick people should be legally allowed to commit suicide, or that unborn babies are disposable, or that it's okay to take foolish chances that put you at increased risk of dying.
- If you recognize that the Lord's Day is sacred, then when Sunday comes around, you won't be so quick to lie out of church, or go about business as usual, or catch up on chores, or get in nonessential extra hours of overtime at work.
- If your tithe is sacred, you'll pay it first, rather than waiting until everything else is taken care of to see if any money is left over.

2. Make the Sacrifice

"But poured it out unto the Lord" (2 Samuel 23:16).

David would have dearly loved to drink the water that his men brought to him. He'd been dreaming of it and longing for it—

You can be absolutely certain that as a Christian, God will call you to make some sacrifices.

even talking about it out loud. Finally, there it was, right in front of him. A nice big jug of his heart's desire, fit to replace the unsavory water he'd been drinking instead. So when he turned the jug upside down and all that precious "blood" water spilled out on the ground, it must have been difficult. This sacrifice really cost David a pleasure he enjoyed. But he gave it to the Lord anyway.

You can be absolutely certain that as a Christian, God will call you to make some sacrifices. You can't just say, "Well, I'm sure glad I don't live in a place where there's persecution," or "I've never really felt called to fast," or "I don't think all Christians have to pray that much." *You have been called to sacrifice yourself*—to give, to pray, to fast, to minister, to devote yourself to His service.

"I beseech you therefore, brethren, by the mercies of God, that ye present your bodies a living sacrifice, holy, acceptable unto God, which is your reasonable service. And be not conformed to this world: but be ye transformed by the renewing of your mind, that ye may prove what is that good, and acceptable, and perfect, will of God" (Romans 12:1–2).

The flesh won't be too thrilled when you make your sacrifice. If you decide to fast, you'll be hungry, and you might feel grouchy or have a headache. If you give to missions when your budget is tight, there might not be enough left over to go to the movies one evening or to buy a new dress. If you volunteer to help with the kids' program at church, you might have to say no when a friend asks you to do something fun on the weekend. But did you pay attention to Romans 12:1–2, above? Sacrificing self leads to "God's good, pleasing, and perfect will." Catch that? It said his *"pleasing … will."* There are some pleasures in life that can only be experienced when other, more mundane and worldly things are let go.

There are some pleasures in life that can only be experienced when other, more mundane and worldly things are let go.

"And he said to them all, If any man will come after me, let him deny himself, and take up his cross daily, and follow me" (Luke 9:23).

Hmm … "deny himself and take up his cross daily" sounds a lot like sacrifice, doesn't it? Flesh needn't be deprived of every good thing forever, but it will have to take a backseat to the spirit on a regular basis if you are truly going to be a disciple of Jesus Christ. Think about it; the rewards are more than worth the price you'll have to pay. Let me explain.

"I am poured out like water, and all my bones are out of joint: my heart is like wax; it is melted in the midst of my bowels" (Psalm 22:14).

David wrote this song as a prophecy of what Jesus would experience at his death. Remember that Jesus quoted the first line of this psalm from the cross, "My God, my God, why hast thou forsaken me?" (Matthew 27:46). This is the same psalm that predicted that people would gamble for Jesus's clothes. "They part my garments among them, and cast lots upon my vesture" (Psalm 22:18).

Isn't it interesting that Jesus's great sacrifice is described as being "poured out like water" by the very man who poured out water before the Lord? The point is that we are called to follow Christ, and no one made a greater sacrifice of self than Jesus Christ. However, wouldn't you say his investment was worth what it cost Him?

3. Shun Lust

"Therefore he would not drink it" (2 Samuel 5:17).

David could have thrown his head back, hoisted that jug of water, and chugged a lug, could he not? He could have let that precious "blood" water run down his face, drunk until he could hold no more, and then wiped his mouth with the back of his hand. But to do so in those circumstances would have been lustful. Lust is simply inordinate desire.

"This I say then, Walk in the Spirit, and ye shall not fulfil the lust of the flesh. For the flesh lusteth against the Spirit, and the Spirit against the flesh: and these are contrary the one to the other: so that ye cannot do the things that ye would" (Galatians 5:16–17).

Many people think of sexual sins when they hear the word "lust," but the term is actually much broader than that. Nearly any fun thing can become an object of lust if desire for it becomes more important than following God's commands. So making the holy choice means to say "no" to things that try to usurp God's place in our hearts.

- Got the urge to go shopping and buy some things you don't need and can't afford? Make a holy decision not to do it, and abstain.
- Feel like engaging in some sort of sexual sin? Is it pulling you ever so strongly to do what your conscience tells you that you should stay away from? Make a holy decision not to do it, and abstain.

"Brethren, be followers together of me, and mark them which walk so as ye have us for an ensample. (For many walk, of whom I have told you often, and now tell you even weeping, that they are the enemies of the cross of Christ: Whose end is destruction, whose God is their belly, and whose glory is in their shame, who mind earthly things.) For our conversation is in heaven; from whence also we look for the Saviour, the Lord Jesus Christ" (Philippians 3:17–20).

Want to eat or drink something that you know very well the Lord would have you leave off? Make a decision not to do it, and abstain.

You have been called to be holy. A holy life necessarily means sacrifice. Discern the sacred, make the sacrifice, and say no to lust. Just do it.

CHAPTER 8

David Insists on Paying for a Threshing Floor

King David only lived to be seventy years old (2 Samuel 5:4), so by the time he was sixty-six, he wasn't far from the end. David had stopped going to battle with his men (2 Samuel 21:17). The vigor and manliness of youth had passed him by. Perhaps he needed to feel strong again, or maybe it was just his ego that needed a shot in the arm.

In any case, David decided to take a census, which is not a sin in and of itself. God had ordered Moses to take a couple, for example (Numbers 1:2; 26:2). But scholars seem to agree that David's attitude and motive for taking his particular census is what got him into trouble with God. David wanted to glory in his fighting men, to say, "What a great nation of warriors I have established!" This way of thinking would be poison to Israel, and there was great sin in David's heart.

And again the anger of the Lord was kindled against Israel, and he moved David against them to say, Go, number Israel and Judah. For the king said to Joab the captain of the host, which was with him, Go now through all the tribes of Israel, from Dan even to Beersheba, and number ye the people, that I may know the number of the people. And Joab said unto the king, Now the Lord thy God add unto the people, how many soever they be, an hundredfold, and that the eyes of my lord the king may see it: but why doth my lord the king delight in this thing? (2 Samuel 24:1–3; see also 1 Chronicles 21)

Joab and his men were just sick. They hated being ordered to do something they knew would get the nation into trouble. But God apparently had in mind to hold the whole nation accountable for something they had previously done wrong. He intended to do so by allowing David to be tempted to take a census and then punishing him and the people for doing so.

Don't be discouraged if certain passages in Scripture seem odd or unfair to you. Don't worry if not everything makes sense the first time you read it. Don't even pretend that you aren't confused. Just read commentaries, meditate on the words, pray for wisdom, and recognize that you won't always understand everything. Take it on faith, and move on.

Here are the things we know for sure: David took a census. It was obvious to his men from the get-go that to do so would be sinful, and they begged him to reconsider. David went ahead anyway. God intended to use the incident to punish Israel for something they had done to displease him.

Notwithstanding the king's word prevailed against Joab, and against the captains of the host. And Joab and the captains of the host went out from the presence of the king, to number the people of Israel. And they passed over Jordan, and pitched in Aroer, on the right side of the city that lieth in the midst of the river of Gad, and toward Jazer: Then they came to Gilead, and to the land of Tahtimhodshi; and they came to Danjaan, and about to Zidon, And came to the strong hold of Tyre, and to all the cities of the Hivites, and of the Canaanites: and they went out to the south of Judah, even to Beersheba. So when they had gone through all the land, they came to Jerusalem at the end of nine months and twenty days. And Joab gave up the sum of the number of the people unto the king: and there were in Israel eight hundred thousand valiant men that drew the sword; and the men of Judah were five hundred thousand men. And David's heart smote him after that he had numbered the people. And David said unto the Lord, I have sinned greatly in that I have done: and now, I beseech thee, O Lord, take away the iniquity of thy servant; for I have done very foolishly. (2 Samuel 24:4–10)

What a shame! David realizes it's wrong and wants to undo it, but it's too late. His men have already spent more than three-quarters of a year going house to house and counting, counting, counting. The climactic moment finally arrives. Referring to their figures, they speak out loud the grand totals as David sits on his kingly throne, eagerly anticipating the results. But once that big number is out, the fun is over. All that's left is an awful sense of guilt. We've all been there. Maybe you didn't take a census, but you succumbed to temptation, sinned, and then felt terrible. But it's not enough to feel remorse. Sin has consequences.

For when David was up in the morning, the word of the Lord came unto the prophet Gad, David's seer, saying, Go and say unto David, Thus saith the Lord, I offer thee three things; choose thee one of them, that I may do it unto thee. So Gad came to David, and told him, and said unto him, Shall seven years of famine come unto thee in thy land? or wilt thou flee three months before thine enemies, while they pursue thee? or that there be three days' pestilence in thy land? now advise, and see what answer I shall return to him that sent me. (2 Samuel 24:11–13)

Oh, the pain of it!! David must choose his poison. And it's not just he who will be suffering for his sin. It's also the people he was so proud of ruling. They're the ones whose crops will not produce for three years, or whose land will be invaded by bloodthirsty enemies, or whose bodies will be ravaged by some plague. How to choose? *How to choose?*

"And David said unto Gad, I am in a great strait: let us fall now into the hand of the Lord; for his mercies are great: and let me not fall into the hand of man. So the Lord sent a pestilence upon Israel from the morning even to the time appointed: and there died of the people from Dan even to Beersheba seventy thousand men" (2 Samuel 24:14–15).

If David wasn't already showing his age, this would do it. Seventy thousand people perished because he insisted on a foolish ego-stroking that his advisors begged him to pass up! This man that the Bible describes as being "after God's own heart" (1 Samuel 13:13–14) certainly had his flaws, didn't he?

"And when the angel stretched out his hand upon Jerusalem to destroy it, the Lord repented him of the evil, and said to the angel that destroyed the people, It is enough: stay now thine hand. And the angel of the Lord was by the threshingplace of Araunah the Jebusite. And David spake unto the Lord when he saw the angel that smote the people, and said, Lo, I have sinned, and I have done wickedly: but these sheep, what have they done?

let thine hand, I pray thee, be against me, and against my father's house" (2 Samuel 24:16–17).

David spoke like a shepherd. He would sacrifice himself to protect his sheep. *Now* we're getting somewhere. David had sinned a great sin, but it was still possible to make holy choices, and he'd finally started moving in the right direction again. The best was still to come, however.

> And Gad came that day to David, and said unto him, Go up, rear an altar unto the Lord in the threshingfloor of Araunah the Jebusite. And David, according to the saying of Gad, went up as the Lord commanded. And Araunah looked, and saw the king and his servants coming on toward him: and Araunah went out, and bowed himself before the king on his face upon the ground. And Araunah said, Wherefore is my lord the king come to his servant? And David said, To buy the threshingfloor of thee, to build an altar unto the Lord, that the plague may be stayed from the people. And Araunah said unto David, Let my lord the king take and offer up what seemeth good unto him: behold, here be oxen for burnt sacrifice, and threshing instruments and other instruments of the oxen for wood. All these things did Araunah, as a king, give unto the king. And Araunah said unto the king, The Lord thy God accept thee. (2 Samuel 24:18–23)

Who wouldn't have made the offer that Araunah did? Here was the king himself, who'd been ruling for over thirty-five years at this point. This king's military might and reputation for being a man of God certainly preceded him. What an honor just to be in his presence! You'd like to buy my threshing floor? Are you kidding? No way! Take it—it's yours! I'm happy to help, not to mention frightened to death of this terrible plague. Let me do my part. I'm making this donation on the spot!

"And the king said unto Araunah, Nay; but I will surely buy it of thee at a price: neither will I offer burnt offerings unto the Lord my God of that which doth cost me nothing. So David bought the threshingfloor and the oxen for fifty shekels of silver. And David built there an altar unto the Lord, and offered burnt offerings and peace offerings. So the Lord was intreated for the land, and the plague was stayed from Israel" (2 Samuel 24:24–25).

It's very important to clear something up here. Fifty shekels of silver (about 1.25 pounds) is not very much. In fact, at 2015 prices, it comes to around $323. The other account of this story is found in 1 Chronicles 21, and it gives some much-needed additional information. The full price for the property was not just the fifty shekels of silver but six hundred shekels of gold, which is around fifteen pounds! At 2015 prices, the gold alone is worth nearly $282,720. So the 1.25 pounds of silver mentioned in 2 Samuel was apparently a down payment, made with cash on hand by men who hadn't expected to make any large purchases and were just carrying around chump change. Then, when David's associates were able to go back to his palace and get the gold, they did so and finished the deal.

Incidentally, this threshing floor and eight acres of property wasn't just any old spot. It happened to be part of a mountain range collectively called Mount Moriah and was the very place where the Torah records that Abraham nearly offered his son Isaac as a human sacrifice (Genesis 22). Later, this land was the site of Solomon's temple (2 Chronicles 3:1), as well as the second temple, which was erected by Ezra (Ezra 6), due to the destruction of the original. Today, it hosts the al-Aqsa Mosque and the Dome of the Rock, the third holiest shrine in the Islamic faith. The Old Testament foretells that when the Messiah comes, he will reign from a temple on this site. (Christians understand this as the second coming of Christ.) The desire of Orthodox Jews to construct a third temple in fulfillment of prophecy on the site of the original is one reason for the great contention between Muslims and Jews in the Holy Land.

What It All Means

Is this story of David's expensive purchase of a place to sacrifice about paying for our own sins? By no means! David did not "pay for" his sin with some silver and gold. He demonstrated repentance through obedience to God's command. So if David wasn't buying off God, why was it necessary for him to make a sacrifice after sinning? Couldn't he just accept God's forgiveness and move on? How was buying the land a holy act? Allow me to answer by beginning with more questions.

Would you want to be in a committed relationship—a friendship, a parent/child relationship, a marriage—where the other person didn't have to give anything of himself or herself? Where the other person had to expend no effort at all for you and never had to show that he or she cared? Where the relationship was completely "take" for him or her and completely "give" on your part? How could you ever really know whether that person cared for you for any reason other than what he or she got out of you? Likewise, would you want your children to never have to show that they appreciated you, or cared for you, or were willing to do anything for you in return for your sacrifice?

How can you give yourself to him?

Quite simply by making a sacrifice.

Good relationships are give and take. We have nothing of value to offer God that isn't his already, except ourselves. God gave himself for us; now he expects the same in return. How can you give yourself to him? Quite simply by making a sacrifice. Some are called to sacrifice their very lives. Some feel called to take vows of poverty, chastity, and obedience. Of one thing you can be sure: even if you aren't called to die a martyr, or spend your life being poor, or stay single, you *are* called to obey. And obedience is often a great sacrifice indeed.

"And Samuel said, Hath the Lord as great delight in burnt offerings and sacrifices, as in obeying the voice of the Lord? Behold, to obey is better than sacrifice, and to hearken than the fat of rams" (1 Samuel 15:22).

Sacrifices are gifts to God that should cost something dear— time, money, or effort.

"What? know ye not that ... ye are not your own? For ye are bought with a price: therefore glorify God in your body, and in your spirit, which are God's" (1 Corinthians 6:19–20).

Acceptable sacrifices come from the best a person has to offer and cost something like time, money, or effort. They should be offered in reverence, obedience, and humility.

> A son honoureth his father, and a servant his master: if then I be a father, where is mine honour? and if I be a master, where is my fear? saith the Lord of hosts unto you, O priests, that despise my name. And ye say, Wherein have we despised thy name? ... Ye said also, Behold, what a weariness is it! and ye have snuffed at it, saith the Lord of hosts; and ye brought that which was torn, and the lame, and the sick; thus ye brought an offering: should I accept this of your hand? saith the Lord. But cursed be the deceiver, which hath in his flock a male, and voweth, and sacrificeth unto the Lord a corrupt thing: for I am a great King, saith the

Lord of hosts, and my name is dreadful among the heathen. (Malachi 1:6, 13–14)

God did a great thing for David and the people of Israel. He turned away his fierce wrath, had pity on them, forgave their sin, and spared them from total destruction. David's obedience in making the necessary arrangements to offer a sacrifice on the altar was a holy choice that demonstrated faith. It is exactly what is needed today too.

What has God done for you? Has he saved your soul? Fed your body? Put loving relationships with good people in your life? Clothed you? Provided you with a good job? Given you a place to live and a comfortable bed to sleep in? Sustained your life to this point? You probably couldn't make a list of everything he's done for you if you sat and wrote for a week straight. Now, answer this: what are you doing for *him*? He made the ultimate sacrifice to redeem you. What are you sacrificing in return?

It might be time to give up small sins, like juicy gossip, white lies, lustful thoughts, laziness, or selfishness when it comes to giving to the local church. It might be time to put in some effort with a ministry to which you've been called. Perhaps the Spirit has been dealing with you about something, like spending more time in prayer. Obey the voice of the Lord. Make the sacrifice He's calling you to make.

If you're a Christian, you're in a give-and-take relationship with the Savior of your soul. Make a holy choice today.

CHAPTER 9

Mary, Sister of Martha, Listens to Jesus

We come now to a very short story in the *New* Testament about making a holy choice. A single adult woman named Mary seemed to be living with her single adult sister, Martha, and perhaps also their brother, Lazarus. They were from the small town of Bethany, which was near Jerusalem. Some Christian scholars believe this Mary is the same as Mary Magdalene, while others disagree, but that is not important to our discussion.

> Now it came to pass, as they went, that he entered into a certain village: and a certain woman named Martha received him into her house. And she had a sister called Mary, which also sat at Jesus' feet, and heard his word. But Martha was cumbered about much serving, and came to him, and said, Lord, dost thou not care that my sister hath left me to serve alone? bid her therefore that she help me. And Jesus answered and said unto her, Martha, Martha, thou art careful and troubled about many things: But one

thing is needful: and Mary hath chosen that good part, which shall not be taken away from her. (Luke 10:38–42)

Can you hear Martha's frustration in her address to Jesus, and can you relate at least a little bit? Jesus was probably traveling with his disciples. Putting a meal on the table for a dozen or so people is no small task, even today, with modern appliances, convenience foods, mixes, and take-out food. Imagine starting from scratch, with no running water, no gas or electric stove or oven, no mixer, no food processor. There was a fire to build, water to haul, bread dough to knead, fresh food to chop, and perhaps even chickens to kill, pluck, and cut up. Martha must have felt her irritation grow by the second as she stood or kneeled at the work surface in her kitchen, alone. "What is wrong with my sister Mary? How can she be so selfish? Who does she think she is, sitting in there with the men, like she's some kind of student of the Law? How unfair! I'm not going to put up with this for one more minute!"

And then there was Mary. The woman dared to step out of the kitchen when she was one of the hostesses and actually spent time talking to this extraordinary man about things from the Law and the prophets. She humbly sat at his feet, like a beginning student, looking up in order to make eye contact—quiet, and listening, listening, listening. Her heart was hungry, and she drank in with great relish the knowledge Jesus dispensed. Mary was making a holy choice.

But to paint Mary as the perfect, spiritual one and Martha as the shallow, earth-minded one may be too simplistic and, frankly, inaccurate. Martha was a fine woman who had many good qualities that Scripture clearly bears out. She eagerly received Jesus into her home (Luke10:38), and she then proceeded to serve him (Luke10:40; John 12:2). It was Martha who later went to Jesus when their brother Lazarus died, while Mary stayed at home (John 11:20, 30). Martha verbally expressed her faith in Jesus's ability to meet needs (John 11:21–22), and she professed that she believed in bodily resurrection and eternal life (John 11:23–27). Finally, she confessed that Jesus was the Christ and God's Son (John 11:27), and she carried Christ's message to Mary (John 11:28). Surely these wonderful qualities that were demonstrated later didn't suddenly appear after the incident in Luke 10. This loving believer is who Martha was.

It may be as important, then, to understand what this story is *not* saying as it is to understand what it *is* saying. In light of other Bible passages, we can ascertain that the story does *not* mean that Mary needn't have helped Martha. Jesus never approved of selfishness or an attitude that seemed to say, "I'm better than you and deserve to be served." To the contrary, His message was about putting others first, denying self, and making sacrifices.

Neither does the story mean that Martha should not have bothered with a meal for her guests or shown hospitality. In fact, on an earlier occasion, Jesus visited Simon the Pharisee and even took him to task because Simon did not show Jesus the customary courtesy of seeing to it that Jesus's feet were washed (Luke 7:44). If Jesus's critics described him as a "winebibber" and a "glutton" (Luke 7:34), we can only infer that he enjoyed sitting down to a nice meal with his hosts. If he didn't think food was important, he wouldn't have fed the five thousand by multiplying bread and fish (Matthew 14:13–21; Mark 6:31–44; Luke 9:10–17; John 6:5–15).

Another thing that Jesus was *not* saying is that only spiritual things really matter. No one was more focused on ministry and his mission than Jesus, but he used some of his very limited time on earth to attend a wedding (John 2:1–11) and to get away with his disciples to rest (Mark 6:31).

What the story *is* saying to us is this:

1. Separate the important things from the vital things.
2. Don't allow the important things to crowd out the vital things.
3. A relationship with God must come before service to Him.

1. It's necessary to separate the *important* things from the *vital* things. The meal for the guests mattered, but Jesus's teaching mattered more. Honoring the guests by serving them was noble, but it honored Jesus even more to sit at his feet and drink in His life-changing Word. There would still be time to get the food on the table.

A balanced and happy Christian life is one in which priorities are clear. The big things at the top of the list must get more time and attention than the lesser things at the bottom.

2. Mary's holy choice also reminds us that we should never allow important things to crowd out vital things. There are only so many hours in a day. Mary knew that Jesus would not be at her house forever. She could spend the brief hours of his visit in the kitchen, trying to make a good impression by putting on a beautiful table, or she could make the most of this rare opportunity and hear what he had to say while he was there to say it. A balanced and happy Christian life is one in which priorities are clear. The big things at the top of the list must get more time and attention than the lesser things at the bottom.

"Therefore take no thought, saying, What shall we eat? or, What shall we drink? or, Wherewithal shall we be clothed? (For after all these things do the Gentiles seek:) for your heavenly Father knoweth that ye have need of all these things. But seek ye first the kingdom of God, and his righteousness; and all these things shall be added unto you" (Matthew 6:31–33).

Did you pick up on that last line—"all these things shall be added unto you"? It's really not as though you have to choose between service and relationship. If you prioritize a relationship with the Lord, time to serve him and even leisure time to do fun things will follow. Put him first, and a reasonable, balanced schedule will fall into place. Really!

3. Mary also demonstrated that a relationship with God must come before service to Him.
Teaching a children's Sunday school class is a fine thing, but if your time is spent preparing for that event to the exclusion of personal devotions and prayer, you've missed the point. Go back to the beginning, gain a new

Put knowing him above doing things for him.

perspective, and restructure your schedule. Just *be* with him for a while. There'll be time to get the children's class ready too. *Put knowing him above doing things for him.*

"And in the morning, rising up a great while before day, he went out, and departed into a solitary place, and there prayed" (Mark 1:35).

"And it came to pass in those days, that he went out into a mountain to pray, and continued all night in prayer to God" (Luke 6:12).

Jesus had a lot of ministry to do, and he had only a scant three and a half years or so to accomplish it. People were waiting. Throngs of sick folk needed to be touched, but he chose to devote a significant amount of time to prayer alone anyway. Are you trying to serve him without really knowing him?

"One thing have I desired of the Lord, that will I seek after; that I may dwell in the house of the Lord all the days of my life, to behold the beauty of the Lord, and to enquire in his temple" (Psalm 27:4).

King David understood the concept hundreds of years before Mary. He had a nation to rule, wars to fight, and a rather unruly family to parent. Yet he took the time to praise the Lord, write songs to the Lord, and visit the spot where the ark of God was being kept (since the temple had not yet been built).

To better understand Mary's point of view and apply it to today, ask yourself which is more important—the house or the people who live there? The food or the people to whom you're serving it? The Lord or the work you're doing for him? Your nice new car or the kids who ride in it? When priorities are in place, it's much harder to "strain at a gnat and swallow a camel."

The holy choice is the one that puts God first—not service to him first but God himself. How beautiful is the righteousness of choosing to give God the place in your life that he deserves.

CHAPTER 10

A Widow Gives Her All in the Offering

The temple that stood in Jerusalem during Jesus's earthly lifetime was the second of two temples to be built on that spot. King Solomon built the first one, after Solomon's father, King David, bought the land from Araunah the Jebusite to offer a sacrifice (see chapter 8). That first temple was built about 960 BC and lasted for some four hundred years, until it was destroyed when the Babylonians invaded Judah. This second temple was built about seventy years after the destruction of the first one. The prophet Ezra and some other Jewish exiles from Judah returned to Jerusalem and did the noble work.

In Jesus's day, Israel was not a sovereign state, and it had not been one since the Babylonian invasion of Judah in 586 BC. The land of Palestine was ruled by Rome's emperor, Caesar. Caesar installed local under-kings in various places to keep order long distance, and the ruler of the area around Jerusalem was generically known as Herod. The Herod of Jesus's day began to govern about thirty-three years before Jesus was born, and one of his pet projects was to restore, refurbish, and add on to the beautiful second temple. He did this to curry favor with the locals so they would accept him. Herod spent about thirty years making a large complex around the temple. It included a place for women, a place for lepers, and even a barbershop for men who had taken a Nazarite vow and were finally ready to cut their long hair (Numbers 6:18). The whole area had a wall around it, a portion of which still stands today and is known as the Wailing Wall, where Jews and others go to pray and place written prayer requests in the cracks between the wall's blocks.

Recall that only priests were permitted inside the temple, and no one went into the Holy of Holies where the ark of the covenant was *at all*, except for the high priest, once a year (Leviticus 16:1–17). So the temple was not like our modern concept of a church, where people go to sit on a pew and hear a sermon. The Jews had synagogues for such a purpose, but the temple was for ritually offering sacrifices and observing the other requirements of the Law. Common people stood outside, surrendering their animals for the Levites to inspect and prepare and also to pray.

One day Jesus and his disciples were outside the temple, not far from a depository for coin offering. Mark records the story (see also Luke 21:1–4).

> And Jesus sat over against the treasury, and beheld how the people cast money into the treasury: and many that were rich cast in much. And there came a certain poor widow, and she threw in two mites, which make a farthing. And he called unto him his disciples, and saith unto them, Verily I say unto you, That this poor widow hath cast more in, than all they which have cast into the treasury: For all they did cast in of their abundance; but she of her want did cast in all that she had, even all her living. (Mark 12:41–44)

Wealthy people were giving to the temple in Jesus's day, just as they still give to churches and charities now. What were some motivations they may have had? Like today, some were probably very noble, giving out of obedience to God's command or the noble conviction that what they had to offer really was needed and would do a lot of good somewhere. Perhaps some felt guilty for the nice things they possessed, and giving an offering helped to assuage the conscience. Some may have felt an obligation to somehow repay God, or fate, or the society that afforded them such a luxurious life. Some may have been eager for the approval of others or even considered charitable giving a kind of investment, expecting that the positive public relations they gained from their gifts would be more than worth the cost. It is easy to think of many reasons, both good and not so good, for a rich person to give to the work of God.

But the difficult question from this story is this: why did the widow woman give? She was very poor, so she didn't have money to spare. In fact, Jesus plainly stated that she put in "everything—all she had to live on" (Mark 12:44). The coins that she put in would have done so very little to promote the work of God, especially in comparison to the other gifts that were given, that the difference between her giving and not giving would surely have been imperceptible. So why did she do it? Couldn't those coins have been used to buy a bit of flour to make some bread?

Life hadn't been too kind to the widow. Where was God when her husband died? Where was this woman's provision if everything belonged to God, and He "owns the cattle on a thousand hills" (Psalm 50:10)? What possible reason would this woman have for giving to God out of her need?

Perhaps the Old Testament prophet Habakkuk can help to answer the question. He wrote a book of warning about the time that Babylon, under King Nebuchadnezzar, was getting ready to invade Judah. The picture would not be pretty, but note his own take on the time of trial and testing.

"Although the fig tree shall not blossom, neither shall fruit be in the vines; the labour of the olive shall fail, and the fields shall yield no meat; the flock shall be cut off from the fold, and there shall be no herd in the stalls: Yet I will rejoice in the Lord, I will joy in the God of my salvation" (Habakkuk 3:17–18).

Isn't Habakkuk's God-inspired attitude the same one that the widow woman demonstrated by her giving? It just doesn't have to be all sun and roses for a person to praise or honor the Lord.

Note also what Job said when times were so tough for him.

"Then Job arose, and rent his mantle, and shaved his head, and fell down upon the ground, and worshipped, And said, Naked came I out of my mother's womb, and naked shall I return thither: the Lord gave, and the Lord hath taken away; blessed be the name of the Lord" (Job 1:20–21).

As discussed in chapter 2, Job did not seem to feel that God owed him anything when he made this statement. The widow too, when she refused to cling to the only pitiful coins she had, was simply saying, "Everything I have belongs to God." May He be praised.

It's not too challenging to praise the Lord with a bit of your excess when you're luxuriating in blessings. Who wouldn't pop a twenty-dollar bill into the church treasury during missions' emphasis week if he'd received a generous bonus or a promotion? Who'd refuse to purchase a fund-raiser candy bar from church youth if he had an extra dollar in his pocket? It's certainly fine to do so, but where is the difficult, holy choice in that? Where is the sacrificial heart of service that glorifies God when times are not so easy?

A person with a true heart for God is not swayed from giving to him by tragedy; not swayed by the death of a spouse or grinding poverty or any other hardship.

The lesson of the widow is simple. A person with a true heart for God is not swayed from giving to him by tragedy; not swayed by the death of a spouse or grinding poverty or any other hardship.

God is good all the time. He has a plan, even when it is not apparent. We can see his plan for the widow, because we have the power of hindsight. God orchestrated it so that Jesus and the disciples would appear at the temple near the coin drop at the very moment that the widow came by. Peter remembered what Jesus said about her, and his recollections later were recorded by his understudy, John Mark, in the first gospel written, Mark. The Gentile evangelist and physician Luke probably relied on Mark's gospel as a template for his own expanded writings about Jesus, and he included the story, too. So for the past two millennia or so, wherever the story of Jesus is read, people have heard about the holy choice this daughter of Israel made. Out of her hardship has come inspiration and blessing. Jesus was so pleased by what she did that God, no doubt, saw to the lady's needs after she gave.

Are you in a time of trial? Are times a little rough at the moment? Don't fail to give to God. He is always worthy, and he deserves your all. Make the holy choice to surrender your whole self to him. What could be better than knowing you have pleased the Master?

CHAPTER 11

Stephen Becomes the First Christian Martyr

The year is about AD 35. Jesus's resurrection was roughly six years ago. The gospel has not yet been preached to the Gentiles.

> And in those days, when the number of the disciples was multiplied, there arose a murmuring of the Grecians against the Hebrews, because their widows were neglected in the daily ministration. Then the twelve called the multitude of the disciples unto them, and said, It is not reason that we should leave the word of God, and serve tables. Wherefore, brethren, look ye out among you seven men of honest report, full of the Holy Ghost and wisdom, whom we may appoint over this business. But we will give ourselves continually to prayer, and to the ministry of the word. And the saying pleased the whole multitude: and they chose Stephen, a man full of faith and of the Holy Ghost, and Philip, and Prochorus, and Nicanor, and Timon, and Parmenas, and Nicolas a proselyte

of Antioch: Whom they set before the apostles: and when they had prayed, they laid their hands on them. And the word of God increased; and the number of the disciples multiplied in Jerusalem greatly; and a great company of the priests were obedient to the faith. And Stephen, full of faith and power, did great wonders and miracles among the people. Then there arose certain of the synagogue, which is called the synagogue of the Libertines, and Cyrenians, and Alexandrians, and of them of Cilicia and of Asia, disputing with Stephen. And they were not able to resist the wisdom and the spirit by which he spake. Then they suborned men, which said, We have heard him speak blasphemous words against Moses, and against God. And they stirred up the people, and the elders, and the scribes, and came upon him, and caught him, and brought him to the council, And set up false witnesses, which said, This man ceaseth not to speak blasphemous words against this holy place, and the law: For we have heard him say, that this Jesus of Nazareth shall destroy this place, and shall change the customs which Moses delivered us. And all that sat in the council, looking stedfastly on him, saw his face as it had been the face of an angel.

Then said the high priest, Are these things so? And he said, Men, brethren, and fathers, hearken; The God of glory appeared unto our father Abraham, when he was in Mesopotamia, before he dwelt in Charran, And said unto him, Get thee out of thy country, and from thy kindred, and come into the land which I shall shew thee. Then came he out of the land of the Chaldaeans, and dwelt in Charran: and from thence, when his father was dead, he removed him into this land, wherein ye now dwell. And he gave him none inheritance in it, no, not so much as to set his foot on: yet he promised that he would give it to him for a possession, and to his seed after him, when as yet he had no child. And God spake on this wise, That his seed should sojourn in a strange land; and that they should bring them into bondage, and entreat them evil four hundred years. And the nation to whom they shall be in bondage will I judge, said God: and after that shall they come forth, and serve me in this place. And he gave him the covenant of circumcision: and so Abraham begat Isaac, and circumcised him the eighth day; and Isaac begat Jacob; and Jacob begat the twelve patriarchs. And the patriarchs, moved with envy, sold Joseph into Egypt: but God was with him, And delivered him out of all his afflictions, and gave him favour and wisdom in the sight of Pharaoh king of Egypt; and he made him governor over Egypt and all his house. Now there came a dearth over all the land of Egypt and Chanaan, and great affliction: and our fathers found no sustenance. But when Jacob heard that there was corn in Egypt, he sent out our fathers first. And at the second time Joseph was made known to his brethren; and Joseph's kindred was made known unto Pharaoh. Then sent Joseph, and called his father Jacob to him, and all his kindred, threescore and fifteen souls. So Jacob went down into Egypt, and died, he, and our fathers, And were carried over into Sychem, and laid in the sepulchre that Abraham bought for a sum of money of the sons of Emmor the father of Sychem. But when the time of the promise drew nigh, which God had sworn to Abraham, the people grew and multiplied in Egypt, Till another king arose, which knew not Joseph. The same dealt subtilly with our kindred, and evil entreated our fathers, so that they cast out their young children, to the end they might not live. In which time Moses was born, and was exceeding fair, and nourished up in his father's house three months: And when he was cast out, Pharaoh's daughter took him up, and nourished him for her own son. And Moses was learned in all the wisdom of the Egyptians, and was mighty in words and in deeds. And when he was full forty years old, it came into his heart to visit his brethren the children of Israel. And seeing one of them suffer wrong, he defended him, and avenged him that was oppressed, and smote the Egyptian: For he supposed his brethren would have understood how that God by his hand would deliver them: but they understood not. And the next day he shewed himself unto them as they strove, and would have set them at one again, saying, Sirs, ye are brethren; why do ye wrong one to another? But he that did his neighbour wrong thrust him away, saying, Who made thee a ruler and a judge over us? Wilt thou kill me, as thou diddest the Egyptian yesterday? Then fled Moses at this saying, and was a stranger in the land of Madian, where he begat two sons. And when forty years were expired, there appeared to him in the wilderness of mount Sina an angel of the Lord in a flame of fire in a bush. When Moses saw it, he wondered at the sight: and as he drew near to behold it, the voice of the Lord came unto him, Saying, I am the God of thy fathers, the God of Abraham, and the God of Isaac, and the God of Jacob. Then Moses trembled, and durst not behold. Then said the Lord to him, Put off thy shoes from thy feet: for the place where thou standest is holy ground. I have seen, I have seen the affliction of my people which is in Egypt, and I have heard their groaning, and am come down to deliver them. And now come, I will send thee into Egypt. This Moses whom they refused, saying, Who made thee a ruler and a judge? the same did God send to be a ruler and a deliverer by the hand of the angel which appeared to him in the bush. He brought them out, after that he had shewed wonders and signs in the land of Egypt, and in the Red sea, and in the wilderness forty years. This is that Moses, which said unto the children of Israel, A prophet shall the Lord your God raise up unto you of your brethren, like unto me; him shall ye hear. This is he, that was in the church in the wilderness with the angel which spake to him in the mount Sina, and with our fathers: who received the lively oracles to give unto us: To whom our fathers would not obey, but thrust him from them, and in their hearts turned back again into Egypt, Saying unto Aaron, Make us gods to go before us: for as for this Moses, which brought us out of the land of Egypt, we wot not what is become of him. And they made a calf in those days, and offered sacrifice unto the idol, and rejoiced in the works of their own hands. Then God turned, and gave them up to worship the host of heaven; as it is written in the book of the prophets, O ye house of Israel, have ye offered to me slain beasts and sacrifices by the space of forty years in the wilderness? Yea, ye took up the tabernacle of Moloch, and the star of your god Remphan, figures which ye made to worship them: and I will carry you away beyond Babylon.

Our fathers had the tabernacle of witness in the wilderness, as he had appointed, speaking unto Moses, that he should make it according to the fashion that he had seen. Which also our fathers that came after brought in with Jesus into the possession of the Gentiles, whom God drave out before the face of our fathers, unto the days of David; Who found favour before God, and desired to find a tabernacle for the God of Jacob. But Solomon built him an house. Howbeit the most High dwelleth not in temples made with hands; as saith the prophet, Heaven is my throne, and earth is my footstool: what house will ye build me? saith the Lord: or what is the place of my rest? Hath not my hand made all these things? Ye stiffnecked and uncircumcised in heart and ears, ye do always resist the Holy Ghost: as your fathers did, so do ye. Which of the prophets have not your fathers persecuted? and they have slain them which shewed before of the coming of the Just One; of whom ye have been now the betrayers and murderers: Who have received the law by the disposition of angels, and have not kept it. When they heard these things, they were cut to the heart, and they gnashed on him with their teeth. But he, being full of the Holy Ghost, looked up stedfastly into heaven, and saw the glory of God, and Jesus standing on the right hand of God, And said, Behold, I see the heavens opened, and the Son of man standing on the right hand of God. Then they cried out with a loud voice, and stopped their ears, and ran upon him with one accord, And cast him out of the city, and stoned him: and the witnesses laid down their clothes at a young man's feet, whose name was Saul. And they stoned Stephen, calling upon God, and saying, Lord Jesus, receive my spirit. And he kneeled down, and cried with a loud voice, Lord, lay not this sin to their charge. And when he had said this, he fell asleep. (Acts 6:1–7:60)

Stephen was a godly man who became one of the first deacons in the early church. Two preconditions for the office he filled were set by the twelve disciples as they looked for help with the daily ministration to the needs of the Christian widows. The conditions were that the men chosen be (1) full of the Holy Spirit, and (2) full of wisdom. The events that led Stephen to become the church's first martyr clearly bear out a life filled with the Spirit. Certainly, to be filled with the *Holy* Spirit is to behave in a holy way, is it not?

Note the seven evidences that Stephen was filled with the Holy Spirit:

1. Of honest report
2. Wisdom
3. Faith
4. Power
5. Presence of God
6. Courage
7. Love

Each of these seven descriptions came about as people observed Stephen's actions, which were based on holy choices. Let's examine each one.

Of Honest Report (Acts 6:3)

A person who is of honest report has built up a reputation over time. That means Stephen must have consistently followed through on what he promised to do, again and again. He must have been trustworthy with money, and he must have been a person who didn't shade the truth or spin the facts to suit his point of view. Our holy God is a God of truth (Psalm 31:5; John 14:6), and people who follow in that vein will make others around them feel secure. Being "of honest report" is the opposite of being a swindler or a hypocrite. Holiness is marked by honesty.

Wisdom (Acts 6:3, 10)

Wisdom is "street smarts" or practical knowledge. Stephen knew what action was appropriate for a particular occasion, which was why he was a good choice for managing distribution of goods to widows when there was a suspicion of unfairness. But beyond wisdom for the job of the day, Stephen had an understanding of the whole of the gospel message. In his sermon to the crowd on the day that he died, Stephen summarized the story of the Israelite people and God's ultimate purpose for them in bringing the Messiah into the world. Note that his message included these key events:

1. Rejection of Moses at age forty
2. Rejection of Moses at age eighty
3. Persecution of the prophets
4. Idol worship that led to exile
5. Murder of the messianic prophets
6. Murder of the Messiah himself
7. Rejection of the gospel

As Stephen understood how all the negatives in Israel's history were leading up to God's offering of salvation to the world, he was able to rationalize the difficult sacrifice of laying down his life for the cause. He also made a powerful case for Christ to his listeners. In the same way, a holy life today should be marked with the wisdom to do the fitting and practical thing and with an understanding that can be shared with others of God's good news to man.

a holy life today should be marked with the wisdom to do the fitting and practical thing and with an understanding that can be shared with others of God's good news to man.

Faith (Acts 6:5)

Faith is belief that is backed up with actions. Stephen's trust in God was obvious to people because of the way he lived his life. Without faith there can be no pleasing God at all (Hebrews 11:6), so it is an essential part of holiness. Do you merely say you have faith in God, or are your actions good evidence that you're certain God exists and will reward you for seeking him?

Power (Acts 6:8)

Acts 1:8 says that Jesus told his disciples they would receive power after the Holy Ghost came upon them. Acts 6:4 talks about the "wonders and miracles" that Stephen did. Then, Stephen preached a sermon powerful enough to incite the rage of the religious leaders of his day and to incite them to stone him to death. Christians who are full of the Holy Spirit should demonstrate the same power, whether they are living with persecution or not. Does the Holy Spirit of God prompt you to witness? Do you live a confident, "on purpose" kind of life for him?

Presence of God (Acts 6:15)

Those whose lives are free from sin, made holy by the blood of Christ, and marked by right choices will experience the presence of God. Of course, God is everywhere all the time anyway, but a holy heart leads to a special awareness of nearness to him. Stephen's experience of God's presence was marked by a shining face as he breathed his last. Remember when Moses's face shone after his time with God on Mount Sinai as he received the Law (Exodus 34:29–30)? Has sin blocked your perception of God's nearness, or can you feel his presence around you?

Courage (Acts 7:56)

Courage is a partner to the power mentioned above. It is an appropriate boldness or freedom from fear. Stephen died bold, not weak, pitiful, and crying out in pain. As Christ courageously laid down his life for us, so Stephen courageously laid down his life for his faith. A holy courage it was! Are you living a brave Christian life? Are you intimidated by those who would challenge your faith? Do you fear going against the crowd to do the right thing? Put on holy courage.

Love (Acts 7:60)

Stephen's ultimate motive for serving as a deacon and preaching the gospel to the disbelieving crowds was love. He loved God, and he loved the people God created who so needed a Savior. As Stephen lay dying, he called upon God to forgive his murderers, just as Christ had done on the cross (Luke 23:34). Real love is holy and seeks God's highest and best will at all times. Is your life characterized by love? Is it obvious to others that you do what you do because you really care for God and others? Remember that Paul described love as greater than even faith and hope (1 Corinthians 13).

Being filled with God's Holy Spirit will surely lead you to make holy choices. Your lovely life will be characterized by the same seven traits that set Stephen apart and made him an excellent deacon and sainted martyr. Does God's Spirit indwell you?

CHAPTER 12

Paul Acts as Peacemaker

When Jesus was just a small boy, a Jew named Saul from the tribe of Benjamin was born outside the land of Palestine in the city of Tarsus, located in modern Turkey. Young Saul was educated in the Torah and became a Pharisee, or religious lawyer. He was also trained in the trade of tent making. Only a few years after Jesus's death and resurrection, between AD 33 and 36, Saul the Pharisee was actively involved in persecuting people of the Jewish faith who held that a certain Jesus of Nazareth was their long-awaited "Anointed One," or Messiah. One day while Saul and some associates were on their way to the Syrian city of Damascus to arrest some of these Jewish "troublemakers," Saul had a supernatural experience with this very Jesus that resulted in his radical conversion to the Christian faith. He began to go by the name of Paul, and after water baptism, study, and conferring with church leaders, Paul set out to preach the gospel of Jesus to the Gentiles of the Roman Empire.

Nearly thirty years later, Paul found himself in prison in Rome for his preaching. This stint in captivity was not to be his final one before being martyred, but while he was there, Paul wrote a letter of encouragement to some believers he had probably never visited, the church at Colosse. This congregation apparently was started by someone who had heard the good news in nearby Ephesus and went on to spread the word in neighboring Colosse. The group of Christians began to meet in the home of a man named Philemon. Philemon was well off enough to have slaves.

In addition to writing a letter to the whole church that met in Philemon's home, Paul wrote a personal letter to Philemon himself. According to tradition, the woman mentioned at the beginning of this letter was Philemon's wife, Apphia. The other man mentioned, Archippus, is thought to be the adult son of Philemon and Apphia, who lived with them and pastored the church.

Paul wrote the book of Philemon as a plea for mercy on behalf of a runaway slave, who'd gone from Philemon's home in Colosse to Rome and then somehow encountered the incarcerated apostle Paul and came to a saving knowledge of Christ. Rome had about 1.5 million people at that time. What an amazing meeting the Lord had arranged! Paul convinced this slave, whose name was Onesimus, that he needed to return to his master and make things right. Paul hoped that sending a letter with the slave would help to smooth the way for a possible reconciliation.

> Paul, a prisoner of Jesus Christ, and Timothy our
> brother, unto Philemon our dearly beloved, and fellow
> labourer, And to our beloved Apphia, and Archippus
> our fellowsoldier, and to the church in thy house:
> Grace to you, and peace, from God our Father and the

Lord Jesus Christ. I thank my God, making mention of thee always in my prayers, Hearing of thy love and faith, which thou hast toward the Lord Jesus, and toward all saints; That the communication of thy faith may become effectual by the acknowledging of every good thing which is in you in Christ Jesus. For we have great joy and consolation in thy love, because the bowels of the saints are refreshed by thee, brother. Wherefore, though I might be much bold in Christ to enjoin thee that which is convenient, Yet for love's sake I rather beseech thee, being such an one as Paul the aged, and now also a prisoner of Jesus Christ. I beseech thee for my son Onesimus, whom I have begotten in my bonds: Which in time past was to thee unprofitable, but now profitable to thee and to me: Whom I have sent again: thou therefore receive him, that is, mine own bowels: Whom I would have retained with me, that in thy stead he might have ministered unto me in the bonds of the gospel: But without thy mind would I do nothing; that thy benefit should not be as it were of necessity, but willingly. For perhaps he therefore departed for a season, that thou shouldest receive him for ever; Not now as a servant, but above a servant, a brother beloved, specially to me, but how much more unto thee, both in the flesh, and in the Lord? If thou count me therefore a partner, receive him as myself. If he hath wronged thee, or oweth thee ought, put that on mine account; I Paul have written it with mine own hand, I will repay it: albeit I do not say to thee how thou owest unto me even thine own self besides. Yea, brother, let me have joy of thee in the Lord: refresh my bowels in the Lord. Having confidence in thy obedience I wrote unto thee, knowing that thou wilt also do more than I say. But withal prepare me also a lodging: for I trust that through your prayers I shall be given unto you.

There salute thee Epaphras, my fellowprisoner in
Christ Jesus; Marcus, Aristarchus, Demas, Lucas, my
fellowlabourers. The grace of our Lord Jesus Christ
be with your spirit. Amen. (Philemon 1:1–25)

Paul made the beautiful and holy choice to serve as a
peacemaker between Philemon and Onesimus. Jesus commented
on peacemakers in his famous Sermon on the Mount. "Blessed
are the peacemakers: for they shall be called the children of
God" (Matthew 5:9).

The techniques Paul used in his attempt to convince Philemon
that he should forgive and free Onesimus showed wisdom and
inspiration, and they serve as a wonderful guide for Christians
today who might have an opportunity to help people who have
had a misunderstanding to find their way to peace once again.

1. Appreciate the Positive

Paul began his letter by acknowledging and giving genuine
thanks for what was already right in Philemon's life.

"I thank my God, making mention of thee always in my
prayers, Hearing of thy love and faith, which thou hast toward
the Lord Jesus, and toward all saints; ... For we have great joy
and consolation in thy love, because the bowels of the saints are
refreshed by thee, brother" (Philemon 1:4–5, 7).

What a great way to disarm someone who might be defensive
or unreceptive to negotiating a truce after a breach! Applying
this kind of praise does not mean using flattery to manipulate
someone. Flattery is just another word for lying. Instead, Paul
found something for which he could genuinely thank Philemon,
and he complimented the good work Philemon was doing. No
one wants to be approached and immediately criticized or
admonished. Start with something positive, and mean it. It is
the right foot with which to step off.

2. Ask, Don't Demand

Another savvy thing Paul did as he worked to make peace between Philemon and Onesimus was not to use his spiritual authority to demand that Philemon forgive. He pleaded, and he implored instead.

> Wherefore, though I might be much bold in Christ to enjoin thee that which is convenient, Yet for love's sake I rather beseech thee, being such an one as Paul the aged, and now also a prisoner of Jesus Christ. I beseech thee for my son Onesimus, whom I have begotten in my bonds: Which in time past was to thee unprofitable, but now profitable to thee and to me: Whom I have sent again: thou therefore receive him, that is, mine own bowels: Whom I would have retained with me, that in thy stead he might have ministered unto me in the bonds of the gospel: But without thy mind would I do nothing; that thy benefit should not be as it were of necessity, but willingly. (Philemon 1:8–14)

People don't like to be dictated to, even in the church. Philemon was not a very young man if he had a grown son, and he must have been fairly well off financially to have had slaves. What good would it have done for Paul to approach this older, successful man with orders? Even if Philemon had complied with Paul's demands, he likely would have resented Paul for being heavy-handed. Paul was wise to ask. If you have the chance to make peace between people at some point, you'd be wise to humbly ask them too.

3. Offer to Make Restitution

"If he hath wronged thee, or oweth thee ought, put that on mine account" (Philemon 1:18).

Who wouldn't be moved by Paul's offer to pay back Onesimus's debt himself? What a Christlike and holy thing to say! Onesimus broke the law. According to the customs of his day, he deserved to be punished for taking off and leaving his master as he did, in a land where slavery was legal and based not on racism but on a person's financial condition. Why would Paul be willing to take Onesimus's debt on himself and repay Philemon, if necessary? Perhaps it was because Jesus had done the same thing for him!

"All we like sheep have gone astray; we have turned every one to his own way; and the Lord hath laid on him the iniquity of us all" (Isaiah 53:6).

Surely it is a holy choice to follow in the footsteps of Christ, the Prince of Peace, by working for peace between others.

Surely it is a holy choice to follow in the footsteps of Christ, the Prince of Peace, by working for peace between others. What an offer Paul made! Perhaps you could speed along the peace process between some of your friends or members of your family if you offered to help repay whatever debt has been incurred. If you hesitate—because you didn't make the mess and don't deserve to have to clean it up—just remember what Jesus has done for you!

4. Have Faith in a Good Outcome

Paul was not in a position to have a face-to-face conversation with Philemon, so he couldn't immediately gauge Philemon's response to the proposal for peace that Paul was making. But

Paul had faith that Philemon would respond positively, and he communicated that faith in his letter.

"Having confidence in thy obedience I wrote unto thee, knowing that thou wilt also do more than I say" (Philemon 1:21).

"I know you'll do the right thing" is a powerful thing to say to someone who is at a crossroads and trying to decide how to react. Although the Bible itself doesn't say what Philemon did after he read Paul's letter, some of the ancient church fathers, including Jerome, recorded that Philemon forgave Onesimus and granted him his freedom. Onesimus then went on to become the bishop of Ephesus, after Paul's protégé, Timothy. Onesimus was eventually tortured and martyred in Rome during the reign of the emperor Domitian in the year AD 90. What a powerful outcome for the kingdom of God! What an amazing chain of events Paul set in motion by choosing the holy role of peacemaker between two people who were estranged!

In short, God is a God of peace. It pleases him when Christian brothers and sisters get along with each other. King David said it best: "Behold, how good and how pleasant it is for brethren to dwell together in unity! It is like the precious ointment upon the head, that ran down upon the beard, even Aaron's beard: that went down to the skirts of his garments; As the dew of Hermon, and as the dew that descended upon the mountains of Zion: for there the Lord commanded the blessing, even life for evermore" (Psalm 133:1–3).

What if you could be personally responsible for bringing about beautiful unity like this? Would that not be a holy and well-pleasing investment of your time for the Lord? Ask him today how you can be a promoter of peace.

EPILOGUE

Remember that holiness is an essential characteristic of almighty God himself. We can never will ourselves to be holy by doing a good thing or by taking the high road here or there. True righteousness of heart can only be imputed when the blood of Jesus Christ, which was shed for our sins, is allowed to wash us and make us clean.

The choices we make after the Lord saves us and makes us his children, however, are up to us, and they can be right or wrong, holy or evil. Have you been inspired by the wonderful decisions men and women from the Bible made when they came to a crossroads? Can you learn from their victories and have wonderful victories of your own?

God will provide opportunities for you to glorify him. You need only make the right choice.

"But as he which hath called you is holy, so be ye holy in all manner of conversation; Because it is written, Be ye holy; for I am holy" (1 Peter 1:15–16).

You have a beautiful heavenly Father. Do you look like him? You can resemble him more every day as you grow in making holy choices.

ABOUT THE AUTHOR

Sarah J. Breese McCoy is an adjunct professor of anatomy and physiology in Tulsa, Oklahoma, and has been a Bible teacher at Owasso First Assembly for over thirty-five years. A lifelong native of Oklahoma, she has been married to Thomas F. McCoy since 1986, and the couple has six children. Sarah enjoys the Spanish language, flying, and playing the flute and piano.

CPSIA information can be obtained
at www.ICGtesting.com
Printed in the USA
FSOW02n1506021115
12874FS

9 781512 714753